Down Right
JOY

TONY D'ORAZIO

Tony D'Orazio
Jacobsladderfitness.com
Ordering Information:
For details, contact tdorazio@att.net

Print ISBN: 978-1-09836-401-4
eBook ISBN: 978-1-09836-402-1

Printed in the United States of America on SFI Certified paper.

First Edition

Dedication

Thanks to the Lord God for making us and giving Jake to Karen and me.

Thanks to our parents Lou and Grace and a great extended family of caring and Christian people for helping us in our journey.

Thanks to the volunteers who serve Jacob's Ladder Special Needs Fitness.

Thanks to all the students in the special needs community who exercise and pray with us and who always seem to give me energy and put a smile on my face.

Thanks to Jake for working hard, being a good example, and helping us serve others.

Acknowledgements

Thanks to my wonderful wife Karen for her support and patience.

Thanks to Karen Ellicott for patiently editing this book and for sharing her insights regarding content, and for her encouragement.

Special thanks to photographer Stacy Jantz for helping with the photo layouts and for the great cover picture of Jake that she took. She also enthusiastically helped me get this book ready to publish. Could not have done this without her. Jantz Photography, Avon Lake, Ohio Jantzphotography@gmail.com

Table of Contents

Foreword

Little did I know how my world would change when I walked into that kindergarten room so long ago. I can do this, I thought to myself as I looked at the little boy sitting at his seat. I had to admit, he could not have looked any more adorable than he did. He had on a plaid collared shirt, little khakis, and the cutest round glasses I had ever seen. He was a peanut. Probably one of the smallest students in the class. I sat down on the little chair next to him, feeling huge and in control. He did not acknowledge my presence at first. He just sat quietly listening to his teacher. I could hardly take my eyes off of him. He truly was one of the cutest kids I had ever seen. And then it came. The look I would come to know. The look that would remind me that I was not one bit in control of the situation. The look that would tell me this little, adorable peanut was in control. As he turned his head and raised his eyes above his round glasses, he looked not just at me, but through me, letting me know that no one or anything was going to tell this boy that he was not the one in charge.

I had never really known anyone who had Down syndrome. I don't mean I had not met anyone or had not seen anyone, but I had never really, truly known someone with Down syndrome. I am not sure, when I look back, what I honestly thought about Down syndrome. I do think that I thought I would have the upper hand. I mean I was not the one with Down syndrome. I did not have the disability, right? This was my first mistake. The word "disability" has no place near the words "Down syndrome." The little boy I met that day, looking so frail and vulnerable, would change my world. Through Jacob, I learned to see the world in a way I had never seen it before. My world would be sometimes frustrating, but immensely more joyful than I could ever have imagined.

Laurie Beetler

Special Education Aide

Muraski Elementary

Introduction

This book is meant to encourage all parents of children with Down syndrome and other special needs. The focus is on Down syndrome because that is our experience, but much of what is here can apply to experiences with other special needs individuals. I especially want to speak to newer parents, because you may initially feel overwhelmed and in need of some good counsel. But more experienced parents can also gain insight here, especially as it relates to physical movement, exercise and expectations.

There are truly a lot of challenges to raising and caring for a special needs individual. In the case of an individual with Down syndrome, these may include physical and mental issues, as well as the whole social acceptance thing. I believe that parents of special needs people may understand as well as anyone what it is like to not be accepted because of the way someone might look. We therefore look beyond the challenges towards opportunities for our children.

Like many of you, our own journey has been challenging, and many times early on, we were not sure what to do. But there is another part of the journey that has been joyous and humorous and has allowed us to laugh, bond as a family, and just plain have fun together. As I say later in this book, you just can't make this stuff up!

We are Christian people who have asked for the Lord's guidance throughout. We do know that God was and is at work here. Each chapter, therefore, ends with a hopefully pertinent Bible verse, then a section entitled "For Consideration." These are things for you to think about that are relevant to the chapter story and possible actions to follow up on. If you are not a Christian or have no religion at all, I will wager that you can still enjoy this book, and hopefully gain some good counsel from what is presented here. Warning: some of these stories are almost PG.

Bible Verse: "…Do not grieve, for the joy of the Lord is your strength." Nehemiah 8:10

For Consideration: To encourage you on the joyful journey and give you a little idea of what might lie ahead, please allow me to share some true stories of the downright joy that Karen, myself, and our entire family have felt with our son Jacob.

Chapter 1

The Lovely Lady

A very attractive and tanned blonde with nice legs is strolling on a sultry, warm summer night, making her way through a crowded bar. She is recently divorced and her sister Nancy has dragged her out to have some fun with their cousin Audrey. Karen had been married for several years, but things had not worked out. She was feeling blue. So she figured, "What the heck. What could possibly happen?" Turns out this night would end up changing Karen's life profoundly, forever and eternally, and in ways she could never imagine or dream about.

Earlier in her life Karen would have welcomed the invitation. She and Audrey had done some mischief together. They were friends as well as cousins. That night, Nancy knew her sister needed to relax a bit, so she insisted that Karen join her with Audrey and some of Audrey's coworkers from St. Vincent Charity Hospital.

I was one of Audrey's friends from work who they were meeting that night. I had never met Karen and did not even know Audrey had a cousin. I had been single for about five years and wanted to meet the right person.

On that beautiful summer Friday evening, we were meeting in the Flats. In the early 1990s the Flats in Cleveland was the place to be, especially in the summer. Bars on both sides of the river, pleasure boats running up and down and across the river, streets filled with thousands of young and not-so-young adults having fun. We were at the Powerhouse, maybe the coolest, or hottest, and most crowded bar in the Flats. Summer weather, hundreds of people, nice-looking ladies. Great place to be if you were single.

I had a suit on from work. We wore suits and ties back then, almost every day. I was cool. Early in the evening at the Powerhouse I had that "ahh" moment when I scoped out a very pretty blonde way across the room on the other side of the bar. She had curly, long hair flowing down over her shoulders. I think it was called "mall hair" back then. Nice tan, pretty eyes, confident with a hint of vulnerability. She was pretty and dressed very classy. I spent a few seconds gazing at her. She was far across the room and, of course, did not notice me in the huge crowd. That was it.

A few hours later, I met Audrey. We were sitting at a booth with several other people, talking, laughing, and so on. There were some people in the booth behind us, and at one point Audrey turned to me and said, "Oh, Tony, I'd like you to meet my cousin Karen." I turned around and—there she was! The pretty-eyed blonde with the curly hair and great tan. OMG! Except we did not say OMG back then. For me it was more like, "Sweet Jesus, it's her!"

Even though Karen had been kind of dragged out that evening by her sister, she seemed to be having fun, and had a few beers. We talked a bit, exchanging pleasantries and information about what we did for work—just some normal conversation. I was thrilled.

I of course thought I was the business stud in the suit and that she would be interested in dating me. So on Monday I called Audrey to see if I could get Karen's number. Audrey called Karen and told her that the guy she met was interested in going out with her and wanted her number.

For this part of the story, I imagine Karen is a blonde southern belle with a sweet southern drawl. And when her cousin mentions me, Karen's eyes get really wide and she says in a very enthusiastic and maybe louder-than-normal beautiful southern voice, "You mean that strapping, broad-shouldered, hand-some, athletic Eye-talian guy with the great suit? Yes, tell that youngster I can't wait to hear from him!"

4

Well, it was pretty close to that. Karen said to Audrey very matter-of-factly and in a monotone voice, "I don't remember him at all." She confessed to a few beers and had no clue as to even what I remotely looked like, let alone any conversation we had.

I was a stud muffin.

We did make it to the first date. We went to the Flats again. She again looked terrific, in dressy shorts and a suit jacket, and she still had that tan. We walked along the river and got to know each other a bit. She held my hand. Her hand and personality were warm, strong, and sincere. That was it for me. She also drove a sporty T-top Camaro. Months later she told me she was upset because I did not try to kiss her on the first date, but that is another story.

We were married in 1993. We almost did not get married because of the children issue. I had two children, Ray, who was grown-up and living on his own, and Jessica, my then teenage daughter who lived with her mom in the Cleveland area. I did not want to have any more children; I was in my 40s and did not want to start all over. I recall one summer night we broke up. I remember her walking up her driveway, and I thought that was it.

Well, she couldn't live without me—or something like that. I proposed to her at St. Malachi Church in Cleveland. We loved each other and wanted to get married. So I said, "OK, let's do this, and whatever happens happens." Just maybe it was one of those prayers like, "Dear Lord, your will be done regarding the children issue with me and Karen."

But inside, I really thought that my odds were really good. Karen had tried many different methods many times to have children and did not succeed. So I thought I was good to go. Marry this wonderful pretty lady and live happily ever after—no more kids!

What I really did not have a clue about was how much Karen really wanted a child, and more than that, the effect of the powerful prayers of her mom and dad. And, even more than that, what the Lord's plans were.

The Hot Tub

We were married for six years and had given up on all the ways to have a baby when Karen turned 40. She was disappointed, but decided to move on. She said something like, "OK, I'm not going to have a child. Let's get a hot tub." A hot tub? Wasn't there a movie called *Hot Tub Time Machine*? I think Eddy Murphy did a routine about hot tubs.

So what does a man do in this situation? Your wife wants children. She apparently can't have any. She is bummed. She turns 40. A hot tub is the perfect gift that says I am sympathetic to the situation and feel bad for my wife. So get the hot tub and let's have fun.

It was a big hot tub that seated six. It was great to have friends over, or to be alone together in it. About six months post hot tub set-up, Karen was pregnant.

Bible Verse: "We may make our plans, but God has the last word." Proverbs 16:1

For Consideration:

- It is amazing how the good Lord moves in our lives if we are open to new possibilities.

- For potential conception help, call 1-800-Hot-Tubb.

Chapter 2

The Birth of Jacob D'Orazio, August 29, 2000

Jacob's birth was premature by six weeks. He was due in October, but came in late August. The birth itself was fairly normal, especially for me. I didn't do anything. Karen was the one in pain. At the birth, the team did not indicate to us that Jacob had Down syndrome. That is probably medical protocol.

The next morning, Karen was by herself when another doctor came to speak with her. He was not present at the birth, but was called in due to the premature nature of the birth. Here is a summary of what he said to Karen, in a nonchalant monotone, as if he was reading directions on how to operate a blender, or was a person without interest or zeal reciting the Pledge of Allegiance.

He said something very close to this; "It is 99% sure that your child has Down syndrome. The good news is that years ago mothers would leave their mongoloid babies at the hospital to be institutionalized. He will never drive a car and may never learn to read or write, but things are better than they used to be. The hospital has books you can read on the subject." He might as well have ended his speech with, "Have a nice day." He then walked out.

Karen was sobbing when she called me. I was en route, thinking everything was fine, but I was also on a work call and unable to take her call right away. So she continued crying, and before I called her back, she called her longtime good friend Judy, and continued crying throughout that conversation.

Looking back over that day, I think that maybe this doctor actually had good intentions. He may have been trying to be realistic. But he (a.k.a. Dr. Bedside) showed a lack of basic bedside manner by addressing a new mother who was alone without family at a difficult time. At a minimum, he could have waited until I was there.

At any rate, everything began to change for Karen when she held her only child in her arms, a boy with a head of thick jet-black hair. At that moment, her heart began to change and a lifelong adventure began.

She later admitted to being angry at the Lord, as she said in her heart, "I waited so long and tried so hard. Why me, God?" This feeling would undergo a major metamorphosis as her heart transformed. Jesus and Jacob radically took care of that. A few years later she said, with tears flowing, "How did I get so lucky to have this guy?" and humbly thanked God.

Bible Verse: "As a mother comforts her child, so I will comfort you." Isaiah 66:13

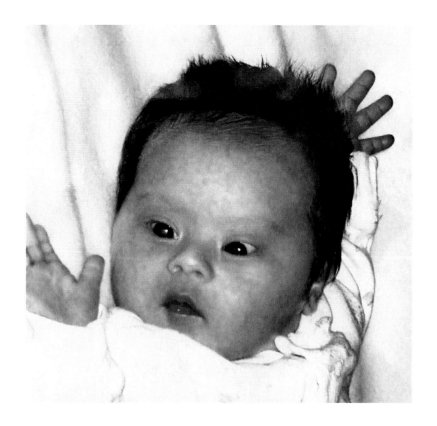

For Consideration:

- Most people are kind and understanding when they talk about having a special needs child. Some, like Dr. Bedside, say the wrong things without thinking, but are not ill-intentioned. In all my dealings with family, friends, acquaintances, and others, I don't think I have ever met anyone with bad intentions. Quite the opposite, people have made tremendous efforts to be nothing but kind and supportive. We are extremely appreciative of that.

- Yes, there will be challenges. Depending on the situation and condition, some of the challenges will be big. However, many of them will be similar to having and raising a typical child. Our young-adult, post-teenage son wants to do what most young men want to do at that age.

- Also, and infinitely more important, is this point for new parents. It is one of the central messages of this entire book. Parents, take a deep breath, gather yourselves. You have a child with Down syndrome. Child and person first, Down syndrome second. This is not a death sentence or a sentence of life imprisonment. You did not do anything wrong. On the contrary, you may be a life lottery winner, or just plain blessed by God.

- You may be overwhelmed at first. That is totally natural. None of us knew quite what to expect very early on. Reach out very early in your child's life to others and to the many organizations available for initial counseling and education specifically related to your child's condition. You will likely find resources in your own area or church, and there are several national and international organizations to turn to for assistance. There are also tremendous people who will serve you and your child. Some have been there and done that and will listen to you and help you in your time of need. Also, begin educating yourselves as soon as you can on your child's particular situation. Become an expert on it. This will help you know what can be expected as you go forward. The resource section at the end of this book has some organizations and contact info that can assist you.

Chapter 3

Goggan

Superman, Batman, and Spiderman are all worthy superheroes. Jake loves them all a lot. Rocky would undoubtedly be his top favorite regular-human movie hero. But by far, Jacob's biggest hero in his early life was Santa Claus. This is no different than millions of kids around the world. That his admiration for Santa still exists into his 20s might be different though!

When he was younger, Jacob called Santa "Goggan" with a short *o*. We don't really know why. From the time he was very young, Santa has been a favorite. I used to think it was because of the gifts, which he likes, but for Jacob, I think it is because of Santa's kind heart and how he loves giving gifts to everyone, especially children.

Many of our Christmastime traditions still involve Santa. For instance, we have all the Tim Allen *Santa Clause* movies, and we watch them repeatedly throughout the season. Jake regularly quotes those movies around Christmastime. He might know the directors of those films better than he does the *Rocky* movies. Don't tell Sly that.

Jacob also includes Santa in our manger scenes. Getting the manger scene up on our hearth is one of Jake's obsessions. It has to be in the exact same place, on the left side of the hearth if you are facing the fireplace. Jacob likes to put Santa right in there next to Jesus, sack of toys and all. There is obviously a strong connection there as well.

Of course, we also still leave food for Santa and the reindeers, and sometimes we try to stay up for Santa.

One of our favorite stories about Jacob and Goggan, a.k.a., Santa, involves an incident that happened when Jacob was about five years old. Karen had to go to her dad's cancer treatment appointment. She put Jake in front of the TV in the first-floor family room and went upstairs to get ready. She was putting her makeup on upstairs. About 10 minutes later Jacob appeared at the bathroom door. He was pretty much covered in fireplace soot from head to toe, His face, arms, and hands looked like he had been power-sprayed with soot.

"Oh my God, what did you do, Jacob?" Mom shouted.

"Mom," Jacob said, almost matter-of-factly, "Mom, I was looking for Goggan."

He had crawled into the fireplace and was trying to find Santa. Yes, he was looking for Santa. Of course, Mom, what did you expect, especially this close to Christmas? Oh, except it was not close to Christmas. Sorry. It was in the summertime. Jacob was thinking ahead. When Karen saw that the light-tan Berber carpeting in the family room had the same deep-black sooty tinge to it as Jacob's face, she may have said a few other things.

Another story took place at Christmastime in our town of Strongsville, Ohio. We took a trip to the mall. SouthPark is the local shopping mall and it was packed with people coming and going everywhere. It is a fairly large mall, over 160 stores, one of those that shoppers come from miles around to get to. Right in the heart of the mall, where all the human traffic is thickest and where the escalators are chock full, is where Santa sits for the Christmas season. There are always long lines and fairly long waits to see him. Luckily, they have a small train that the younger kids can ride before and after their sit-down with the main man.

This day we were in the mall with Jake and were busy shopping like mad fools, along with a few thousand others, and barely noticed Santa as we worked our way up the crowded escalator. We then noticed a familiar person riding

13

alongside us, our neighborhood friend and Karen's cousin Jodi. Like us, she was on a shopping mission. We chatted briefly as we moved upward with the masses.

Then, from just down below us in the center of the mall, Santa called out very loudly in the crowd of hundreds of people who were in the immediate area, "Hi, Jacob!"

We stopped talking, so did several others around us, and many who were closer to Santa. Jodi looked very surprised and looked at us for a second, then said, "Santa knows Jacob?!"

"Yah," we said, not shocked at all. "Of course he does." Jodi smiled, shook her head a bit, and we all moved on with our shopping sprees.

Bible Verse:"But the fruit of the Spirit is love, joy, peace, patience, kindness, goodness, faithfulness, gentleness and self-control." Galatians 5:22

For Consideration:

- Raising any and all children requires patience.

- You can never have too much Santa and Christmas Spirit in your life and home.

Chapter 4

Grandpa Wolf Goes Home

Karen's dad, Ronald Henry Wolf, was born February 1, 1929, at St. Anne's Hospital, Cleveland, Ohio. He grew up on E. 77th Street in Cleveland. He was the middle child of three, with two sisters. He graduated from Benedictine High School and received an associate's degree from Fenn College after serving in the army. Ron was inducted into the army on February 5, 1951, during the Korean War, and was transferred to the army reserve on January 9, 1953. He was honorably discharged on January 23, 1957. He was a private first class stationed in Germany and received the Army of Occupation medal (Germany).

Typical of the Greatest Generation, he served his country proudly, honorably, and without fanfare or calling attention to his own situation. He felt blessed to be alive and well. He had done his duty for his country. He then raised a good family and really enjoyed his retirement.

He was a mechanical draftsman, a perfect job for his quiet but analytical and perfectionist personality. He started work at NASA, where he met his bride-to-be, Betty. At some point he became more than interested in this very pretty assistant who also worked at NASA. The laid-back analytical guy soon figured out this lady was not only beautiful, but available. They were married in 1954. Ron then worked for National Acme Cleveland for 35 years and retired from there in the 1990s. After retirement he worked as a starter at Briarwood Golf Course.

Ron's love was Betty and his family. He also loved golf and bowling. His golf was precise, like his work. He did not hit that far, though he was respectable, but straight was his thing. Had Jacob been the right age, his grandpa would have been his personal golf instructor. But, thanks to many individual golf lessons, Special Olympics golf and coaching from uncles Vince and Dan Jake has become a pretty good golfer. He has the hand-eye coordination and power. If he is hitting straight, he can get very close to 200 yards on his drives. He is not a bad putter either. He does well in Special Olympics golf and can hold his own in a scramble. Grandpa would be proud.

There were crosses to bear though for Grandpa Wolf. His youngest daughter, Nancy, was diagnosed with multiple sclerosis (MS). Grandpa cried when he got this news. Later on, Nancy lived with her dad and mom, and it was a beautiful example of family helping each other.

For Grandpa and G-Ma, Jacob was one of four grandkids. They loved them all dearly. But one of the other times Grandpa cried was when he found out Jacob was born with Down syndrome. He knew we would have to face many challenges. But also, for that generation, having a special needs child was different. They viewed these individuals more sadly; the R word was used.

Nowadays there is much more focus on inclusion and there are all kinds of programs and organizations to assist parents of special needs children. Yet, with all the inclusion and all the programs, today's culture is more savage than ever as a very high percentage of individuals with Down syndrome are aborted in the name of "choice." To those of us blessed with these individuals, this is unthinkable.

As time went on, Ron and Betty got to know Jacob, and we are pretty sure they favored him. Christmas was just plain over-the-top with the number of gifts Jake got from them. We always knew that their hearts were good and they genuinely loved their grandson, especially after they got to know him.

Sometime around 1999 Ron was diagnosed with prostate cancer. He hoped for the best, and had his prostate removed. For several years after that he enjoyed fairly good health. But then his health declined, and eventually he had to face the inevitable. His health continued to decline rapidly and the family knew he would soon pass. On June 18, 2006, Ron went to his home in Broadview Heights to be with his loved ones for the last time. It was where he wanted to be. It was best for him to be with those he loved so much before he went to eternal rest and paradise.

A person dying of any kind of cancer is not a pretty thing. There is a lack of consistent consciousness, speech is limited and often inaudible, and there might be a bad smell. There is a very frail person losing his life. Ron was in a hospital bed that had been tipped up, so he was kind of lying at a 45-degree angle. His mouth was open. His young grandchildren, Nicholas, Jacob, and Matt, were there with their beloved grandpa, but they were upset, and maybe scared, and unable to do much or say anything.

Then, something profoundly beautiful, caring, simple, and spiritual happened. Six-year-old Jacob climbed up on a stool into grandpa's lap and literally put his face right up to Grandpa's face. He looked directly into Grandpa's eyes and began to sing the line from the hymn "Be not afraid, I go before you always, come follow me…." Grandpa looked up, took a deep breath, and died a few minutes later.

Bible Verse: In Matthew 18:10, Jesus called a little child and had him stand among the disciples and said, "See to it that you do not look down on one of these little ones. For I tell you that their angels in heaven always see the face of my Father in heaven."

For Consideration: Jacob was not afraid or thinking about himself. He was focused on his grandpa, and Jesus of course. This sincere act of kindness and deep faith will always be remembered by all of us who were there. Is it possible that some of our children are somehow more connected to the Almighty?

Chapter 5

G-Ma's Little Helper

Elizabeth "Betty"Rung was born on March 14, 1927 in Cleveland. She was the second youngest of six children of George and Anna Rung. She went to John Marshall high school. She worked at NASA where she met her husband Ron Wolf. She also worked at BP in downtown Cleveland and was known as a hard working administrative assistant.

Several years after Karen's dad passed, her mom Betty came to live with us. Affectionately referred to by her family as G-Ma, she was diabetic and it became difficult for Karen's sister, Nancy to care for her. She was with us for about two-and-a-half years before we could not care for her. Then she went into assisted living. She died about a year after that.

Karen is a professional medical assistant with a background in occupational medicine and urgent care. She now works in the cardiac area at the Cleveland Clinic. Her excellent background and skill set made her a very good caregiver for her mom. Karen gave her mom her regular doses of insulin; checked her insulin levels; administered the various drugs she took; and cooked for her, washed her clothes, and took care of her personal hygiene.

Also during her time here, G-Ma and Jacob became very close. Jacob hung out with G-Ma, watched their favorite TV shows and movies with her, and also explained all the *Rocky* and *Superman* movies to her. He became somewhat of a caregiver for her too. Under Karen's very close hands-on supervision, Jake learned to assist in some procedures and became very proficient at it.

His room upstairs was right across from G-Ma's. One winter night Karen went to check in on her mom and discovered Jake in the bedroom. He was concerned about her getting cold and wanted to make sure she was warm. So he put an additional blanket over her while she slept.

For Karen, it was another one of those "how did I get so lucky to have this guy" moments. We got another demonstration of what the Bible calls a "pure heart."

Bible Verse: "Blessed are the pure in heart, for they shall see God." Matthew 5:8

For Consideration: What can we do to foster that kind of heart on a daily basis? Maybe create an atmosphere of caring and help our kids learn to assist and serve others. And, it doesn't get much better than this story.

Chapter 6

Escape Clause

When Jake was about six years old, our Church was expanding rapidly and major renovations and construction were happening at the church. There was a huge ditch/hole in the front of the building where the new worship center was going to be. Inside, there were metal studs where rooms were being built. It was one of those scenarios where you can walk through the walls and visit all the rooms. It was a major construction site, dangerous for an inquisitive and impulsive soul like Jacob. At that time, he always wanted to see what was going on at church and loved exploring the new areas, especially if they were not complete.

One weekend during this construction period, Karen traveled to Atlanta on business. My daughter, Jessica, and I took Jake to church, dropped him off in the childcare area, and went to the service. As part of the construction, the gymnasium/activity center was utilized as the worship center. We sat towards the back of the large gym so that we could easily leave to fetch Jake. There were likely 300 to 400 seats in the gym and it was a packed house that day, as usual.

We almost always saw and talked to Karen's sister Nancy after service, though sometimes we ran into her before. That day we did not look for her before the service. Afterwards, we headed down to pick up Jake, and planned on meeting up with Nancy. When we got to the childcare area, which was a classroom with only one entrance, the volunteer there looked around, then at us, hesitated, and then said, "Jacob is not here."

She said it in a kind of quiet tone, no panic in her voice, kind of like when you make a business call on someone and the very busy administrative person says, "Mr. Jacob is not here right now," very matter-of-factly, as if Mr. Jacob had stepped out for a cup of latte or went to get a bagel.

But Jacob was a young special needs boy with a propensity to sneak out. In this case, he might be sneaking around a large construction site with about 500 people moving about the building on three different levels. Jessica, not being swayed by the nice tone and a young protective mother herself, said matter-of-factly and maybe a little sternly, "Well, where is he?"

Here is what the kind volunteer young lady did not understand, just like the high school swim volunteer did not understand (see "Swimming Angels")… Jacob has skills. He can blend quietly into a group in the classroom before escaping. He will not cause any disturbance, sort of like the invisible man. Then, when the time is right, he will quietly walk/sneak out of a classroom with only one single door entrance. Pretty smart kid.

This blending in and sneaking off happened to Karen and I on a few occasions, including once in downtown Cleveland at a March for Life event. I turned my back for no more than three seconds, and Jacob was gone. I panicked much more in the downtown Cleveland environment than at church. There were many more dangerous possibilities downtown, some of them life threatening. We found him about five minutes later in the Disney store, looking at toys.

But I was still fairly worried at the church that Sunday some 15 years ago, because of all the construction. There was communion that Sunday, which happens near the end of service. Nancy was up towards the very front of the room. After receiving communion, Nancy sat, head down, deep in thought and prayer.

Then she had one of those feelings some people get when they sense someone is there. Even though their eyes are closed and they may be contemplating other things, they get a sense of someone else being there. Or maybe it goes back to her strong connection with Jake. Either way, Nancy lifted her head and looked to her left, and there he was. It was six-year-old Jacob, standing close to her, with the impish smile on his face she knew so well. He had managed to find her among several hundred people.

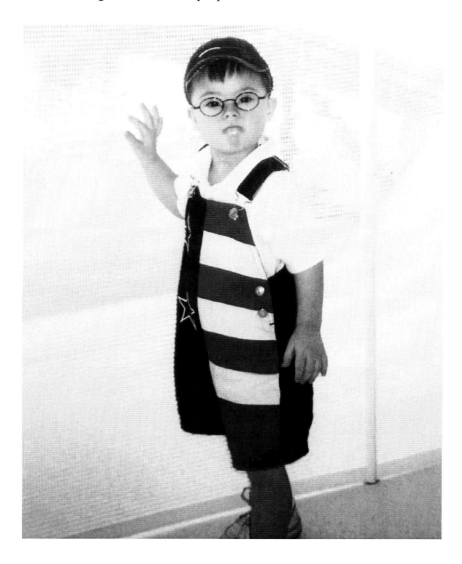

At this point, Nancy assumed I had sent Jake up to see her after getting him out of the childcare area. She then looked around and did not see me or Jessica. She then further assumed I had just left him in the back of the church. Sort of a casual thing, as if I had said, "OK, Jacob, you are on your own, son. Go see Aunt Nancy. We'll catch up later." So, she was kind of mad at me for seemingly leaving Jacob unattended. As the service ended, she began looking for me with Jacob at her side.

Little did she know I had just learned that he was not in childcare and was on a quasi-panicked search for Jacob. In my mind, I knew he would be headed to the construction area of the church and lots of danger. I also knew he had the ability to blend in, to work through large crowds without anyone paying attention to him. Heck, he had just managed to "escape" from a classroom with only one entrance and more than one volunteer present, so getting to the construction area would be no challenge.

Everything turned out well. We ran into Nancy and Jacob after service. We all shared our assumptions and had a good chuckle, sort of. And we discussed how little Jacob managed to find Aunt Nancy in a very large church with several hundred people in the worship center.

Bible Verse: "The righteous person is rescued from trouble, and it falls on the wicked instead." Proverbs 11: 8

For Consideration:

- This may have been said already, but it's worth repeating. Do not underestimate the ability of your child to read situations and work the system.

- Volunteers and caregivers at places you regularly go to, like church, school, gym, etc. should also be made aware of and reminded of this.

Chapter 7

Signage

Jacob was about 12 years old when this story happened.

As parents who want to intentionally raise good children, we know the importance of disciplining our kids. As Christians who want to impart God's love through good discipline, we are charged clearly with this task. In Proverbs we are told in various places about discipline, including the famous line of Proverbs 13:24, "He who spares the rod [referring to any kind of discipline] hates his son, but he who loves him is careful to discipline him." Notice the word "careful."

We are also just as clearly told in Ephesians 6:4 that we should not "exasperate" our children, but instead bring them up in the training and instruction of the Lord. Training and instruction imply encouragement and expectations. So we are to discipline our children because we love them, but not do it in a state of extreme anger or to get back at them. These principles apply to all parents and children.

This is an important backdrop to our discussion and story. I think those of us who are parents of special needs individuals sometimes struggle with this. We want to raise the kids right, but we tend to sometimes feel sorry for them, and as a result, we may let them slide a bit. They may not have as many friends or lack social skills, and therefore have a limited social life. We take that burden on ourselves and try to figure out how we can help, support, and nurture. Therefore, sometimes we cut them some extra slack, and I think that is OK, even good at times. The wisdom part comes in where we have to decide what is right at the time of the incident.

Sometimes 12-year-olds act stubbornly. Would it be fair to say to you parents of individuals with Down syndrome that our kids are stubborn? Might it even be fair to say that our children can be pure butt stubborn at times? OK, I know that you parents in particular understand. Part of this might be the nature of their genetics, part of it might be us not reacting properly, and part might be that sometimes we just need to hold the line, show discipline and love, and follow through on what we say we are going to do. Easier said than done, right? And, don't forget about that other part of their nature—the pure, loving, and caring side.

Jake had been acting stubbornly one day and became very obstinate about not wanting to obey a very simple instruction regarding.... Well, I forgot what exactly it was about.

On that day, I had finally had it, and said to Jake, "Go into your room right now and stay there until I tell you that you can come out!" Yes, I raised my voice and was very stern. But being an experienced former childcare worker and parent to three, I knew that in these situations it is often good for everyone to cool off a bit before making any decisions you might regret later. So I left the situation and went downstairs to take some deep breaths and regroup.

Ten minutes later, I went back upstairs to Jake's room to check on him. I wanted to make sure he was in his room and was OK. When I got to his room, his door was closed and locked. There was a sign on the door that read...

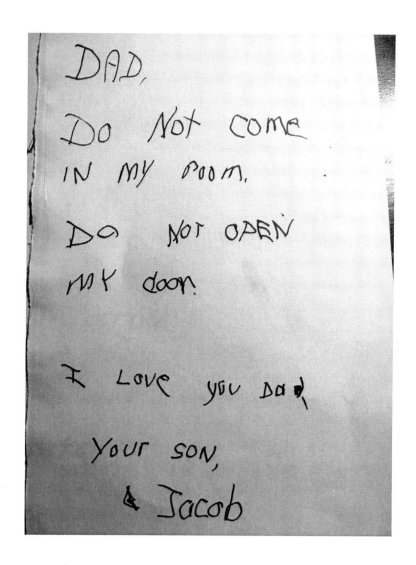

DAD,

Do Not come
IN mY room,
Do Not OPEN
mY door.

I Love you Dad,
Your SON,
& Jacob

Bible Verse: "No discipline seems pleasant at the time, but painful. Later on, however, it produces a harvest of righteousness and peace for those who have been trained by it." Hebrews 12:11

For Consideration: This was one of those many times I smiled, almost cried, and thought, "I love that boy." He did accept his consequences. What a blessing that we have this young man. Many of you out there are agreeing—and smiling.

Chapter 8

The Perfect Christmas Card
By Laurie Beetler,
Special Education Aide

One of my favorite stories about Jacob was a pretty typical day at Muraski Elementary. Now when I share this, I do not want you to get the wrong idea. Jacob was a regular in the principal's office, but it was not always because he had gotten into some kind of trouble. There were many times he wanted to right some injustice that he witnessed or just visit with the principal. They had become very close, and I often witnessed the principal doing everything in her strength to not smile or chuckle when Jacob sat in the chair across from her.

I honestly do not remember what it was that Jacob was sent to the office for that day, but as his aide, I always went with him. The thing with Jacob was, if he did do something that he knew he should not have done, eventually he would become apologetic and humble. Until that point was reached though, he could really give us a runaround. Well, as I recall this particular time, Jacob was very quiet and sorrowful as he sat across from his principal, getting a serious lecture on his recent poor choice.

He sat quietly, staring at the principal and nodding his head in agreement with everything she said to him. My heart almost broke for him, and yet I was so pleased that he really was getting it. He had reached a milestone—being responsible for his actions. What progress we made! It was a day I could go home and know that I had made a difference, that Jacob was really growing.

After the long lecture, the principal asked him if he understood all that was said. Without hesitation Jacob replied that he did. As we stood up and headed out the door, Jacob stopped, turned around, and said to his principal, "You are so beautiful. Your face should be on a Christmas card." Without waiting for her answer, he turned and walked out of the office. The principal said thank you to Jake and acted very calm. After he left her office, she laughed as she shook her head.

Bible Verse: "Put on then, as God's chosen ones, holy and beloved, compassion, kindness, . . . and patience . . .." Colossians 3:12

For Consideration: Much patience is required for all children. And, being able to socially interact with those in authority in a positive way is a valued skill. Not sure Laurie agreed with me on that particular day.

Chapter 9

Taking the Plunge

Jake grew up attending Grace Church in Middleburg Heights, Ohio, with Karen and me. It is a very wonderful Christian church that has grown a lot over the years. Pastor Jonathan and his wife, Mary, are the nicest, most welcoming people you will meet. Jonathan is a skilled and sincere speaker who preaches the gospel of Christ in truth and humility. He is the epitome of 1 Peter 3:15, ". . . Always be ready to give an answer to everyone who asks you to give a reason for the hope that you have, but do this with gentleness and respect."

Grace Church has a large and well-organized special needs respite ministry called Take a Break. We know it is well run because Karen's sister, Nancy (see Chapter 20), helped run that program for many years. As a parent, you can drop your special needs child or adult off there on a monthly scheduled Saturday and leave them there for four hours from 4:30–8:30 PM. During that time, a group of wonderful and dedicated volunteers keeps your child safe and also does various activities, such as crafts, walking, singing Christian songs, and watching good movies or videos with them. They also have various people and groups come in to provide entertainment for the group, such as singing and other activities.

It is usually a one-to-one ratio of volunteers to participants and many great relationships develop. Some of these are long-term friendships that the special needs individuals crave and cherish. Jacob formed several very meaningful friendships with the volunteers over the years.

There was a wonderful young volunteer couple there named Heather and Paul who got to know Jacob pretty well. Often one of them was paired with him. At one point they asked us if they could talk to us about Jake. Sure thing I said. My first thought was OK, what is that little rascal up to? Was he doing or saying something inappropriate? Did he con someone? Would they not want to have him at the respite anymore?

What they said did definitely surprise Karen and me. I think it was Paul who said, "Heather and I are getting married here at the church and wanted to know if Jacob could be our ring bearer for the ceremony." Wow! How nice and sweet and caring and inclusive is that?

So, young Jacob was part of a great marriage ceremony and got to spend a very special day with those he cared for who also cared for him!

One other aspect to this church is that they have immersion baptism. Next to the main stage in the church is the pool where baptism takes place. Those being baptized will often first give a short testimony to the congregation. Then, dressed in casual clothes that they don't mind getting wet, they will proceed to the pool and walk slowly into the water. They are met by a pastor who prays with them, then dips them backwards into the water. Having seen this procedure many times during his life, Jacob was intrigued by the whole process.

Almost every week, Jake would go into the prayer room after the service and pray with those faithful volunteers who take time to minister to others. He would have prayer time and deep conversations about God and his family. He would be there praying and talking for a good 10 to 15 minutes sometimes, and I will admit to occasionally wishing he would not take so long. I should be beaten with a rubber hose for thinking that.

Then, one day at home, 10-year-old Jacob was talking to Karen and me after church and said, "Mom and Dad, I want to be baptized."

We were obviously happy. But then we started thinking (stupid us) and wondering why he wanted to be baptized. We were thinking that he wanted to go into the pool of water, kind of like a short Sunday morning swim. So, being the smart and savvy parents that we are, we asked "Jacob, why do you want to be baptized?" His response was simple and honest. "Because I love Jesus," he said.

"Well," we replied, a little taken aback, kind of being hit to the body with a Rocky hook and realizing how much deeper and more spiritual and simpler he was compared to us, and at the same time being so proud of our boy, "That is a good reason."

That's a good reason! Really? That is THE reason we get baptized, silly parents.

Remember I said in the second chapter how Jesus and Jacob radically changed Karen's heart? Several weeks later, the two of them stood together before the congregation, Karen gave her testimony, and they were baptized.

Bible Verse: "I tell you the truth, anyone who will not receive the kingdom of God like a little child will never enter it." Mark 10:15

For Consideration: The act of kindness by Paul and Heather will be remembered by Jake his whole life.

IQ should not be confused with spiritual awareness. God's word and Jacob's example here speak of the beauty of simple faith. And how about Jake and Mom getting baptized together?

Chapter 10

Swimming Angels

There are about 1.5 million volunteers who are the backbone of the Special Olympics organization nationally. They are coaches, trainers, officials, event organizers, fundraiser hosts, managers, unified partners, and fans cheering in the stands. Our volunteers are all ages and their commitments can range from an afternoon to a lifetime—but everyone who donates his or her time makes Special Olympics possible.

There are parents of typical children who regularly coach a sport, like track. I am thinking of a particular family in Strongsville, Ohio, Coach Dale and his family. He and his wife are coaches, their son is a coach, and the son's wife is also a coach. And they have been coaching for years. No fanfare and no pay, of course. Just honest and patient dedication to the special needs athletes of Strongsville, Ohio. There is also Dave and Gail, a couple who headed up the track and basketball program for Special Olympics in Strongsville at the time of this story. All of these people are truly servants. Parents like me and Karen appreciate and admire their dedication, and so do millions of parents of special needs individuals around the world.

These volunteers also include many thousands of high school students who serve out of the goodness of their hearts. Or, possibly, the need for service hours—probably both, but it's all good.

Being the parent of a Special Olympian and having worked in the special needs community as a coach for many years, I see that sometimes the volunteers are a bit uneasy about what to do and how to communicate with and coach the special needs population. They may be tentative in how they direct and encourage the athletes, mostly because they just don't know and aren't experienced with this population. I think that makes them all the more valuable, as they continue on with sincerely good intentions, even though they may be feeling a bit unsure of what to do in all situations.

This brings us to the next Jacob story.

Karen had Jacob in the water when he was an infant. There was a

aquatic program at Cleveland State University for the special needs population that allowed the children to get exposure to moving in the water early on. So, Jake was used to the water at a very young age.

We decided to have him take swimming lessons when he was about nine years old. This was at the Strongsville Recreation Center. His instructor was

NOT a specialist who exclusively worked with special needs children. In fact, she may never have worked in the special needs population at all. She just taught swimming to kids. She took Jake through the normal swim routines, got him used to the water, and helped him through the various stages of becoming a swimmer.

There was one thing she did not do, and it was something that could have caused us to back away from her if we were different kinds of parents. She did not feel sorry for him.

In fact, in some ways, she seemed to not have that many feelings for him. As I reflect back on that time, I sort of envision her as a Marine drill sergeant swimming coach who said in that excited but stern military tone of voice "That boy will swim!"

In all actuality, she was awesome. She realized early on that Jake was a pretty good athlete. And she did not concern herself with what he could not do. She had expectations for this young man. He would learn to swim. And he did, actually very well.

At one lesson, we were sitting by the side of the pool, observing closely as our son came swimming towards us from the other end of the pool. The water was deep there, at least six feet deep where we sat. Suddenly, he started to falter and flail, his arms kind of beating the water without rhythm. He was struggling. Being a good mom, Karen started to get up to go and grab him, to save her son from almost certain mayhem.

But she was denied. The drill sergeant swim instructor raised her arm, blocking Karen from going to the rescue, then very matter-of-factly said, "He's fine, let him go." Ok, I still think of her as a Marine.

About a second later, Jake recovered and was on his way. He didn't even notice his mom or me. He swam another 20 yards or so and finished his lap, as he was expected to.

Fast forward several lessons and Jake is jumping off the 15-foot high board, then safely swimming to shore, smiling and wanting to do it again. One issue we had with him as he got older was that he would not want to wear his life jacket when we went swimming in Lake Erie, but of course we made him.

He has won several swimming medals at Special Olympics state meets, which are held at The Ohio State University natatorium. (More kudos to the Special Olympics Ohio organization and OSU—awesome stuff!).

Not that long after the swimming lessons from that absolutely wonderful lady who we admired so much, we were at a Sunday morning Special Olympics swimming practice. Same rec center, same pool. The kids were swimming laps, but things were not going smoothly. Lots of kids, lots of volunteers. Coaches were trying to get the kids to swim, and the new volunteers did not know what to do.

There were several first-time volunteers from the Strongsville High School swim team. Some were young lady swimmers in sleek bathing suits. One of them was working with Jake. She had never met Jake, didn't know him from Adam, and for sure did not know he could swim extremely well, or his other skills.

So, there we were, sitting several yards away from the pool, casually watching practice. But not much was happening. The swimmers seemed to be kind of hanging out by the end of the pool, just milling around in the water. And Jake was not swimming either, but he was not just milling around. As Karen got up and walked over to the pool, there was Jake, in the water. He had his arm strategically placed around the young lady volunteer's waist. He was holding her close, like a kid who did not know how to swim. Again, she did not know Jake. It was her first time as a Special Olympics volunteer. She may have thought, "This poor kid with Down syndrome, so nice, so loveable, likes to hug. And the poor dear can barely keep his head above water. I better hold onto him closely."

Karen walked over to the pool, and looked down at Jake. The smile on his face was as wide and bright as an instant lottery millionaire winner. The boy was grinning ear to ear! He was right where he wanted to be.

But the gig was up. "Throw his butt in the water," Karen said. "He swims like a fish!" The volunteer released him and he started swimming quite well on his way down the pool. The volunteer might have thought, "What a mean mom, forcing her 'disabled' boy to swim." Or maybe she observed, "Wow, that little blank really can swim."

Bible Verse: "Isn't he rightly named Jacob? He has deceived me these two times." Genesis 27:36

For Consideration:

- The swim instructor had expectations. She did not look at limitations or a disability. She looked at a student that she would teach to swim. Oorah!

- Get your child in the water early, Jake was in the water before he was a 1 year old. There are many adaptive swim programs for the very young.

- Looking back, I recommend not waiting till they are nine years old for formal swimming lessons.

- Do NOT underestimate your children's abilities related to athletics, or at being con artists. They are pretty good charmers and know how to work the system.

Chapter 11

Jesus and the Man of Steel

People with Down syndrome tend to have tactical issues. Karen and I once attended a seminar put on by a registered nurse who was also the mother of a child with Down syndrome. She explained that these individuals like very soft clothes. As time has passed, we have realized that this is absolutely true. Jake is spot on when it comes to recognizing the softest shirts. There are really soft shirts and not-so-soft shirts. Luckily, Karen has done a great job of finding Jake clothes that are not "itchy" as he puts it. Jake really loves soft, white t-shirts. He especially likes to wear them for several days in a row. Most guys can relate to this. The shirt is just more comfortable after a few days.

Jake is also a huge Superman fan. Just like the *Rocky* movies, he has all the *Superman* movies and knows a lot of the actors and plots. Karen found him the perfect Superman t-shirt, blue with the big red *S* on the front, and very soft cotton. That shirt became one of his main workout shirts. The sleeves were eventually cut off, as they were on many of Jake's shirts. As he outgrew the Superman shirt, he of course kept wearing it. It had been washed 100 times with Mom's best choice for fabric softener—and really was soft.

Then on one sunny summer Sunday morning, we were all getting ready to go to church. Nowadays church dress is very casual and we are OK with that, to a point. We wanted Jake to look nice and be respectful to those in church. So we made the rule that sleeveless shirts were not to be worn to church. We have pretty much stuck to it. As we were leaving for worship service that day, Jake came downstairs with flip flops on his feet, athletic basketball type shorts, and the sleeveless Superman shirt.

Karen and I looked at Jake, then at each other, and she said, "Jake, you know you cannot wear sleeveless shirts to church." She was not angry or shouting, but made our point. Then, something wonderful and funny and maybe deep on a spiritual level came out of Jake's mouth. As he puffed out his chest, he then traced the red letter S with his finger and proudly proclaimed, "But Mom, Dad, the S is for my Savior!"

We were stunned for a second. Nobody coached the lad on this! And there is no way he could have rehearsed it. He came up with that all on his own, right in that moment. No other quick-thinking teenager or seasoned salesperson ever in history came up with a better response in about one second! The response

41

was sincere, though intended to get him what he wanted. Yet it presented the opposition with an alternative that was very close to their hearts, and made them see his side of the equation. He was using Steven Covey's "Win-Win" principle, and his end in mind was clear. He wanted to wear the Superman shirt, and he wanted to make his parents feel good about it.

And, most of all, what he said was true. He does sincerely love Jesus.

I think we were in awe of him for a moment. Then Karen smiled and hugged him and said, "Very nice, Jacob. We love it that you love Jesus. That is awesome! But you need to put a shirt with sleeves on." He complied with some reluctance, but had made his presentation and point.

Bible Verse: "Guide me in your truth and teach me, for you are God my Savior." Psalm 25:5

For Consideration: Enjoy the children you have and be ready to smile and laugh at some of their antics.

Chapter 12

Jacob, Rocky, and Thunderlips

To say that Jacob is a Rocky fan would be a very gross understatement. It would be unlawful to just say Jake likes Rocky. It would be a sin with a small *s*. Since he was able to talk and walk, he has watched, recorded, listened to, talked about, emulated, and totally loved the *Rocky* movie experience. He has the whole collection of *Rocky* movies, with more than one of some of the titles on DVD. He will sometimes ask for newer DVDs of the collection, as he thinks they might wear out. He has also recorded the same *Rocky* movies when they come on TV.

Whenever a new *Rocky* film came out, Jacob and his cousins and friends went to see the movie dressed in Rocky shirts, robes, and other accessories. It was always fun. Jacob watched a heck of a lot of *Rocky* movies in his life. Jacob's audio collection includes the various *Rocky* movie CDs. Now he can just call the *Rocky* tunes up on his phone as he works out.

I think the attraction to Rocky for Jake is on a few different levels. The original *Rocky* is a classic underdog story about a man no one expects much from, including himself initially. He is the total underachiever who at first did not even want to accept the fight with Apollo because he felt completely unworthy. But through extreme hard work, dedication, and trust in his trainer Mick, Rocky comes out on top.

I think Jake is also drawn to Rocky's simple loving and caring personality, as demonstrated by his relationship with Adrian. Rocky was even kind and merciful to his obnoxious brother-in-law Paulie. And Jacob likes the boxing and training aspect of the movies. By learning to hit the speed bag very proficiently, Jake has become very good at a high-end aspect of this sport. This supports a positive self image.

Our basement is pretty much a Rocky gym combined with a man cave and big-screen TV. In our gym there is a heavy bag and speed bag, attached as one unit. Karen got this from her hairdresser friend for $60. The speed bag has a leak in it, so we have to blow it up each day that we use it. That alone is Rocky-like. Jake pretty much taught himself on the speed bag. I did coach him up, but he had the desire from early on.

We also have a treadmill, Trimax machine, Schwinn Airdyne, wrestling mats, lots of dumbbells, resistance bands, a Perfect Pullup bar (which provides a great adaptive version of pull-ups and chin-ups), a Rip:60 workout device, a Ping-Pong table and foosball table. We have gradually added these pieces over the years and the room is pretty full.

The basement/Rocky gym is decorated with about 25 pictures of Rocky. Many years for his Christmas gifts, Jake received Rocky pictures or posters. There is a guy named Bill Pruitt who does Rocky paintings. Karen found him, and we often ordered a picture annually. Aunt Nancy, Uncle Greg, and the rest of the aunts and uncles also get him Rocky pictures and posters. Jake also has the stars-and-stripes shorts, the black-and-gold robe, the stocking caps, and various pairs of boxing gloves. On a non-Rocky note, Uncle Rye got him a pair of signed Buster Douglas boxing gloves and a signed picture of Douglas's knockout of Mike Tyson.

Two of the Rocky pictures are autographed. One is from the original *Rocky* and is framed. One of the early contributors to Jacob's Ladder literally pulled this picture off his office wall and handed it to me. God bless that man. The other picture came from some connection Jacob had in junior high. I cannot recall exactly what it was, but we have a full-sized poster from *Creed II* with three autographs—Michael B. Jordan, Dolph Lundgren, and Sly. There are some really good people in this world.

There are also pictures with Rocky quotes. One is about becoming a champion. "Every champion was once a contender that refused to give up." That is a Rocky Balboa quote. However, there is another poster with a quote and picture of Sly. This quote reads, "The more I go to church and the more I turn myself over to the process of believing in Jesus and listening to His word and having Him guide my hand, I feel as though the pressure is off me now."

In Zechariah 4:6 it says, ". . . 'Not by might nor by power, but by my Spirit,' says the Lord Almighty." This simple verse is packed with the essence and power of the Christian life, which is don't be self-reliant, and don't be puffed up about ourselves, our own things, and our abilities. Instead, allow the Holy Spirit to use you for bigger purposes. This does not mean you don't do anything. It means, "It's not about you!" In other words, Tony, humbly rely on God and strive to do his will. What a concept. We are not the center of the universe!

Jacob is very familiar with this verse, because in the movie *Rocky Balboa*, just before he fights the reigning heavyweight champ, Rocky prays with his old buddy from the first *Rocky*, Spyder Rico. Spyder was a club fighter turned believer in Jesus who worked in Rocky's restaurant. In *Rocky Balboa*, Spyder reads that verse to Rocky. Jake remembers that scene, and who Rocky fought, and who directed the movie. Good way to remember a verse. It was in a *Rocky* movie. Awesome job Sly.

Thunderlips

Most of us Rocky fans remember Thunderlips in *Rocky III* before the fight, when he came into the ring with three women with him and said, "To all my love slaves out there: Thunderlips is here! In the flesh, baby. The ultimate male versus the ultimate meatball."

I don't remember how we found out about the annual Rocky Run in Philly. But in 2014 we heard about it and just had to go to Rocky's hometown, even if it was in the cold of November. Only after we registered did I find out it was put on to benefit Special Olympics in Philly. Jake has been in Special Olympics since he was eight, so that sealed the deal for us, though Jake was already sold as soon as he heard Rocky Run.

What he found more difficult to understand at that time was that, if it was the Rocky Run, why wouldn't Rocky be there? As in, "in the flesh, baby!" It only made total sense of course. He got over that eventually—or he might by the time he is 30, unless he meets Sly. (Where are you Stallion? Jake loves you!)

Getting our Rocky outfits coordinated was a very focused effort on our part. We did our homework, which was not hard for us. We watched the original *Rocky* and saw the Rocky outfit we wanted to copy. We also looked at the various pictures of Rocky we had at the time and did a little online homework. Then we were good to go.

I really don't see how Jake and I did not win the best costume award. Just look at Rocky in the original movie, then look at Jake's pictures from that event. Jake, Rocky, and I all had gray sweatpants and black, old-fashioned Converse high-top tennis shoes (not especially great for running). We also all had lighter gray hooded sweatshirts under a darker gray sweatshirt, which was itself cut off about halfway down the arms. We all had the classic black stocking cap. Jake's hat did have the word "Rocky" on it, but that was because of the extreme popularity of the movie, so I thought he should get some poetic license on that minor issue.

Here is the kicker—the one thing that put Jake head-and-shoulders above all the other Rocky costumes. It was that freaking off-blue towel Rocky had around his neck. Jacob's blue towel matched Rocky's towel the best of any costume ever at the Rocky Run. Period.

And, that blue towel makes sense. A dirt-poor boxer from Philly who was training would not have any money. He would just use any towel he had in his apartment. Nothing would be color-coordinated. He might have gotten it free somewhere. Or maybe Adrian gave it to him from the pet shop. My guess is that it was his kitchen dish towel that he grabbed on his way out the door on a cold Philly morning at about 4:45 AM.

I remember it took some time to find that colored towel at a store. It was a very funky off-blue color, not something Karen or most any other wife would get. But we eventually found a very close match.

We left for Philly on a Friday, the day before the run. It is about seven hours by car from Cleveland to Philly. We stayed at a hotel Rocky might have stayed in, not really nice, but the price was right. Early Saturday morning we got to the race site very early. It was pre-dawn. We took some pics and videos of the Rocky Steps at the Philadelphia Museum of Art and of Jake coming up the steps with his Rocky wig on.

Once people started to arrive, we realized what a large event this was. There were likely 3,000 runners there, most of them dressed in some rendition of one of the characters of the various *Rocky* movies. Some wore clothes from other characters, such as Apollo, Mr. T, and Drago. There was a guy walking around in a suit coat and hat who looked a heck of a lot like Sly. There was a fairly long line to get your pic taken in front of the Rocky statue. And yes, Jake managed to get his picture taken with some pretty ladies who were dressed like Rocky.

Before the race began, the runners gathered near the bottom of the Rocky Steps. *Rocky* music blared out everywhere, interspersed with the loud voice of the race guy, who announced the various groups as we prepared for the run. Everyone was grouped by the times they had given for the various runs—5K, 10K, and other.

As we milled around looking at the various costumes and heard all the renditions of the *Rocky* songs, Jacob found someone who totally made this trip most enjoyable and terrific fun for both of us. Keep in mind it was 34 degrees Fahrenheit. Luckily there was no wind. Still, most if not all Rocky runners had adequate clothing on for the cold, including hats, gloves, and long pants.

But not the guy Jake spotted.

"Dad! Dad," he said running up to me. "You gotta see this." He grabbed my hand. "It's Thunderlips, Dad!"

Remember Thunderlips from *Rocky III*, played by the Hulkster himself, Hulk Hogan? At that time, Hulk Hogan was a strapping, muscular hunk of man at 6' 8" tall and 280 lbs. His biceps bulged. His arms were as big as Rocky's waist. His thighs were sinewy tree trunks, and his yellow Speedo barely covered what it was supposed to. He was just a huge muscular man. Enormous compared to Rocky.

Hulk Hogan as Thunderlips was all man, muscle, and macho. The man that Jake spotted in Philly in 2014 in 34-degree weather had the same kind of Speedo Thunderlips had on in *Rocky III*. But the Speedo looked a little different on this man compared to Thunderlips.

"Dad. Dad, look. He is a plumber!"

Well, there it was. We had a full rear view of this man, with only a tight white Speedo a few sizes too small and clearly showing, well, you get the picture. Remember it was 34 degrees! He also had a blond wig and was holding a balloon-made doll of Rocky, shaking it like it was a rag doll.

Turns out this Thunderlips was actually a balloon artist in the central PA area and also a minister. Yes, the Lord works in mysterious ways. Look closely and you can see some of the detail of the Rocky balloon he is holding. We ended up taking several pictures with this good-natured and under-dressed young man.

Bible Verse (for Rocky): "So he said to me, 'This is the word of the Lord to Zerubbabel: "Not by might nor by power, but by my Spirit," says the Lord Almighty.'" Zechariah 4:6

For Consideration: It would be hard to make this stuff up.

Rocky is the epitome of many special needs people, low expectations with a lot of potential that needs to be harvested. Fitness and training are one way for members of the special needs community to excel and be better at whatever they choose to do.

Chapter 13

A Kindly Note

The special needs aides in our school system and yours are wonderful human beings! They are some of the most influential people who touch our kids' lives. They assist the teachers in the day-to-day, hands-on learning experiences that are so important to the special needs community. Examples of what these folks do include such tasks as assisting in daily learning activities based on the individual education plan (IEP) specific to each student, providing group instruction to a class of special needs students, staying with the students virtually all of the school day, assisting in feeding and bathroom needs, helping students get on the bus, and other duties as needed.

As a result of this and their dedication to these children and young adults, many times the aides are the closest people to the special needs population. Strong relationships are established, just as in the case of our good friend Laurie Beetler and Jacob.

One of Jacob's aides at Strongsville High School was a lady named Kelly. She functioned as an aide in the classrooms and in the lunchroom. Like Laurie and the others, she is a dedicated and caring professional staff member. She had a very good relationship with Jacob and also helped push him along to do better, follow directions, and learn and mature in other ways.

Sometime in late 2019, Kelly's mom passed away. Needless to say, it was a difficult time for her and her family. She grieved for her mom and mourned her loss.

One day at school she got a rather unusual sympathy card from one of her students. It was written on the back of a white paper plate from school. It said:

The note was from Jacob. He felt her sorrow and wanted to let her know that. That seems to be part of his DNA.

A few days later we got a text from Kelly with the picture of the paper plate sympathy card. The text read, "What a kind and thoughtful young man," followed by a heart emoji.

We later saw her on a neighborhood walk and she told us how nice that was, and that he still checks in on her via text every so often.

Bible Verse: "Rejoice with those who rejoice, mourn with those who mourn." Romans 12:15

For Consideration: Karen and I could not be prouder of our son's ability to feel the pain of others and his desire to share their burdens. I am thinking some of your children also have this wonderful quality.

Chapter 14

The Equalizer

Like many of us, I have always enjoyed movies and stories about heroes, especially those who protect children, mothers, and the less fortunate. My recent favorite in this genre is *The Equalizer*, starring Denzel Washington. He plays a retired government operative with years of experience who loses his wife to illness. He is a technology wiz, who is extremely observant down to the slow-motion detail. He is also super good at reading people and situations and has off-the-charts tracking and killing skills, not to mention a certifiable case of OCD.

The movie plot is that he decides to come out of retirement and use his skills to protect a young girl caught up in Russian mafia sex trafficking. He takes pity on her after he gets to know her personally. He gives her hope, and promises her she can lead a better life. He then takes out a whole bunch of really bad guys in order to save her. They are no match for his arsenal of weapons, hand-to-hand combat skills, technical superiority, super intelligence, and focused protective passion.

For many children in the special needs community, there is a time in their lives when they need protection. Jacob was no different. When he was in the middle school age group, this became a real problem. There were several incidents in which he ran off. This happened at church, at school after wrestling practice, and in several other situations. In fact, when I contacted the Strongsville police to get info on the situation I am sharing here, they sent me what they thought I wanted. It was information about another episode in which the police assisted us in finding Jake. Karen and I had forgotten about that situation, probably because it only lasted about 30 minutes.

The incident being relived here was no 30-minute deal. It was a gut-wrenching, fear-for-his-life event lasting over four hours. Imagine for a moment that your young and vulnerable child is lost outside in wet and cold weather. And you feel helpless even though you and the police are searching frantically. That child has been gone for several hours and you can't help but imagine his demise. Who do you call? Who will protect that child?

It was Wednesday, March 19, 2014. Jake was 13 years old, in junior high. The weather was 39 degrees Fahrenheit that night, cold and wet.

The evening began as a routine evening. I was in bed early, like 9:30-ish. Jake was sent to bed a little after Dad. Except he did not go upstairs. He opened the window on the first story of our house, then silently removed the screen and went outside. He crossed the street and went over to our neighbors the Majors. He knocked on their front door and asked Mrs. Major if he could do a sleepover. Bernice Major kindly explained to Jacob that it was a school night and that he could not sleep over. He did not object as she said good night and told him to go home. She carefully watched him walk up to our house across the street and approach the garage door. "OK," she thought, "he is home safe." Then she went inside.

About 20 minutes later, Bernice decided to call Karen, a mom instinct thing, just to be sure Jake got home and inside safely. Upon hearing what happened for the first time, Karen was alarmed, but she thought she would go up and check to see Jacob in bed and everything well. But Jacob was not there. He had never reentered the house.

At 10:22 and 32 seconds PM on that 39-degree March night, just after she came upstairs to wake me up, Karen called the Strongsville police to report Jacob missing.

A few short minutes after that, I was out on my bicycle riding around the neighborhood, since I could cover more ground that way. At the same time, neighbors began to appear and jumped right into the search. Many of them got in their cars and drove around looking for and calling out for Jacob. Others were on foot, searching the cold backyards and places he might be hiding.

The neighbors were just so awesome and helpful. A few of the moms stayed with Karen in the front yard, trying to console, comfort, and pray with her. In total, we were joined by about 50 neighbors and friends and 11 of Strongsville's finest.

I spent some time with the Strongsville Police officers in the canine unit. They came to the house and got Jake's scent from some clothes Karen gave them. They then scoured the wet neighborhoods. The Fire and Emergency Services units used their truck's powerful headlights and thermal imaging cameras to illuminate the many dark wooded areas of the search.

More than a mile from our house, I was riding and searching when some high school kids in a car stopped me and asked if I had seen a young boy named Jacob. They explained he was lost and they were trying to find him. Wow! That was a very beautiful thing. I thanked them, told them who I was, and we all kept searching.

Things frantically ran through my mind, like Jacob being cold. Even though Strongsville is a fairly good-sized city, many of the neighborhood houses are on larger lots and there are a lot of wooded areas around. There are also ravines and creeks in various backyard areas. At that time of the year, there was cold standing water everywhere in backyards and wooded areas. Jake was maybe 100 pounds and under five feet tall. I could not get out of my mind the vision of him somewhere alone and cold.

Then, an even worse thought—coyotes. There were and are regular sightings of coyotes in Strongsville. There are sometimes bulletins and warnings about leaving your smaller dogs out in your backyard. A kid Jacob's size would not be much of a match for a hungry coyote. I did not share this with Karen until days after the ordeal was over, and I still get nervous just thinking about it.

We then heard there was a boy who may have fit the description near the Strongsville town square. I thought I knew then for sure where Jacob was headed—to climb the water tower! He had talked about that many times. He wanted to go up the ladder to the top and hang out by the pictures of the Strongsville Mustang mascot painted on the tower. It did not matter that the area is fenced in securely and the bottom of the ladder is literally 15 feet or more up the water tower. To a frightened and panicked dad, he was halfway up already.

In a short time, the police were at the tower as I was—but no Jacob. There was relief for a few moments, then back to the fear I had for him because of the cold and the waiting coyote that I already had a picture of in my head. This was maybe 11 or 11:30 PM.

Back at home, Karen was vomiting in our front yard. Neighbors continued to pray with Karen that Jacob would be found safely. Everyone prayed for protection and a rescue for Jacob.

Who Are These Angel Beings?

As Christians, we believe that God protects us, and the Bible teaches us that he sometimes uses angels for the job. Research professor of theology and biblical studies and Cambridge PhD Wayne Grudem wrote an entire article on this topic (The youtube version is found at pintrest.com/pin/5733645963110182300). Angels are powerful beings who do God's bidding. The angel Gabriel who stood "in the presence of God" (Luke 1:19) announced to Zechariah the coming of Jesus. Some of these supernatural beings guarded the entrance to the Garden of Eden (Genesis 3:24). Others, like the archangel Michael, are charged to lead God's angelic army in the end times (Revelation 12). He will lead God's army directly against the devil and is referred to as the "first and chief prince" in Daniel 10:12-13. In Revelation 20, John tells us that an angel, presumably Michael, "seized the dragon." These beings are powerful and have been given special powers by God.

In a reference to how much Jesus loves children, he says in Matthew 18:10 that children's angels "always behold the face of my father in heaven."

This says at the very least that Jesus assigns angels to protect children. Angels are also described as "mighty ones who do his work" (Psalm 103:20).

I have always thought that the images and depictions of angels at the resurrection of Jesus were just not very well done or accurate. The angels are always pictured as kind of mild-mannered and gentle beings, not like warriors or protectors.

We know that the Pharisees went to Pilate and asked for a guard to be placed at the tomb. Some biblical scholars believe Pilate gave them a Roman guard (Matthew 27:62–66). A Roman guard is a small unit of 8 to 16 soldiers. We know they had strict orders to obey and were the finest military in the world at the time. Their penalty for failure was death, plain and simple.

A few paragraphs later, Matthew tells us, "There was a violent earthquake, for an angel of the Lord came down from heaven and, going to the tomb, rolled back the stone and sat on it. His appearance was like lightning, and his clothes were white as snow. The guards were so afraid of him that they shook and became like dead men."

So, this angel is assigned the absolutely glorious task by God to go down to earth and roll back the stone on Resurrection Sunday morning and welcome Jesus as he comes out of the tomb. When the angel comes down from heaven, he causes an earthquake. So we know he was exponentially powerful. And I'm thinking he must have been kind of large and heavy to cause all that. He walks right into a group of Roman soldiers who have been given strict orders to guard the tomb of some rebel rabbi.

Think about that for a minute.

Here you are—a Roman soldier. You have heard all the stories and rumors about Christ, which to you are just fairy tales. Then, you start to feel the ground shake fairly violently. You hold your ground, but the shaking is getting closer to your station at the tomb, and it sounds like fairly large footsteps are coming toward you. Coming around the corner of the large rocks that are all around the tomb—there he is! Maybe seven or eight feet tall and massively wide at the shoulders. Possibly wearing armor, or just a robe, but appearing like lightning in color that seems to explode from his being and light up the universe! As he strolls through your unit, the earth continues to shake. His hair is long and flowing, his eyes are focused on the tomb. There is no trace of fear in his eyes as he comes among your squad of armed soldiers towards the tomb. He is almost smiling. His face is kind but resolute. He is not remotely paying any attention to you and your fellow soldiers. You know he is there for a purpose.

If a soldier did try and stop him, he would have gotten a powerful reminder of who was in charge. Perhaps a soldier came up to the angel with sword drawn, and the angel looked at him, and they had one of those "Really?" moments. It could have been that when the soldier approached him, the angel picked the soldier up with two hands, one under each shoulder. Like when a mom picks up her baby who has wet himself and holds him at arm's length in front of her. The angel might have then set the soldier down in a seated position off to the side. The Roman soldier might have indeed had an accident.

As he reaches the stone that seals the tomb, the stone that took five soldiers to roll into place, the angel turns his head towards you and your unit. He looks each of you directly in the eyes, no fear, just purpose. Not one soldier responds. All are in shock, with blank stares. Some faint and fall to the ground. Then, effortlessly, the angel turns and rolls the stone to the side, turns again towards you, and hops up casually and sits on the enormous stone he has just moved. He might have said to the soldiers, "You guys OK if we get ready for the King to come out?" Or maybe he just sat there waiting, maybe with a knee up, an elbow resting on his knee, thumb under chin. That is the last thing you remember before fainting.

So, we are talking about very powerful beings that battle the devil himself, worship God, proclaim God's coming, and protect the little children that Jesus values so highly. Sort of like maybe God's own private and divine Equalizer team, or like a special forces Rambo group. Or, as Jake would say, they are "bad asses."

For us, there is no doubt someone was looking out for Jake on that night he went missing, someone much bigger and more in control than us. Someone who on that night heard the desperate, on-your-knees, begging-and-sobbing prayers of a mother beside herself and losing it in her front yard, and a father searching frantically everywhere on foot and on bicycle, while thinking of the worst possible scenario. Did I mention a fervent and rather stubborn German grandma sitting inside invoking the Lord's assistance? And, on the far west side of Greater Cleveland, a prayer warrior Italian grandma was also doing her thing.

Think about the Bible parable about the persistent widow (Luke 18:1–8). This was a determined lady in need and she was not about to give up petitioning the judge. She just kept asking. Just like her, there was no giving up here in terms of praying for Jacob's safety.

A gracious God heard the many prayers that evening and directed his team to protect Jacob on that cold night. Jacob later told his mom that he had gotten stuck in a creek while trying to cross it. He cried out for help until he lost his voice. He was in a hilly and wooded terrain. He could have easily succumbed to the cold and wet conditions. But his cries were heard. We are so thankful to God for providing this kind of very strong fatherly protection to his family.

It was about 1:15 AM, and I was still cycling around searching backyards, wooded areas, and streets for our son. I spotted a police car in the local Drug Mart parking lot. They were about to deploy the helicopters with the searchlights when we got the news. Jacob found his way to a house about a mile away and smartly knocked on the door. A call was made. The police picked him up and brought him home!

When he came up the driveway after getting out of the police car, I could tell he was frightened by the look in his eyes, a look I had not seen on his face before or since. I also knew he was soaking wet and cold by looking at his clothes. He had his grandma's wool winter coat on with a fur collar, snow pants, and boots. It was all soaking wet and muddy. We had to throw the coat away.

Mom got to him first, of course, and hugged him profusely for a long time. I then took my turn. It was the kind of hug parents give their children who have come back safely from active combat, the kind kids remember forever. Maybe a little like the kind of hug Jesus will give us when we see him, and just before we high five his angels.

Bible Verse: "The angel of the Lord encamps all around those who fear Him, and delivers them." Psalm 34:7 (NIV)

For Consideration: Thanks Lord Jesus! Some of our children have tendencies to want to go on impulse. Consult your doctor and other professionals regarding these issues.

Collier Drive special needs boy found after involved search

Police and fire personnel, area residents comb area

Story   Comments   Image (2)   Share   Print   Font Size

Tweet 0   Like

[Previous] [Next]

Photo by TERRY BRLAS

Missing 13-year-old Collier Drive boy found

The Collier Drive area was the scene of a hunt for a missing 13-year-old special needs boy. The outcome was positive, as the juvenile turned up safe at a neighbor's home following the almost three hour search.

Posted: Saturday, March 22, 2014 9:00 am

By TERRY BRLAS Strongsville Post editor |
0 comments

Posted on Mar 22, 2014
by Terry Brlas

STRONGSVILLE – A harrowing situation had a happy outcome for city of Strongsville safety forces, one Collier Drive family and a community of individuals that leapt into action the evening of March 19.

A 13-year-old special needs boy was reported missing by his mother at around 10:30 p.m. The juvenile had snuck out a front window of his home to go to a neighbor's house for a sleepover. His mother told him it was a school night and to come home.

The Strongsville police K-9 unit, Strongsville Fire & Emergency Services personnel, and area residents assisted in the search.

"We take a call like this very seriously so the supervisors designated every available resource," said Mark Fender, Strongsville deputy police chief. "All this stuff is going on and additional resources are involved."

Chapter 15

Two Honest Men

We simply do not as men, always live up to the standards of purity set forth by the Lord, even though our faith in Jesus is very important and central in our lives. Our parents taught us about Christ and we made our choice to follow him. Christ is there to help us follow him, forgive us when we fall short, sometimes allow us to live through the consequences of our behavior, and point us back in the right direction, towards him.

This story takes place when Jacob was about 17 years old. As mentioned, we attended Grace Church in Middleburg Heights, Ohio, for several years. We also talked about Pastor Jonathan. His dad, Donald Schaeffer, started Grace Church at a small site a few miles from the current site. Wonderful man, humble, godly, knew the Bible well.

I had the unique privilege of being in a small Bible study group with Pastor Donald. This was probably in the late 1990s. I'll never forget that one of our study discussion topics was about the issues of sex, lust, and rock-and-roll. I think the pastor was about 70 at the time.

I asked the question, "Pastor, at what point in your life were you able not to have any lustful thoughts, not be tempted at all in that area, and be free of this burden that affects us men?"

I was waiting for something very profound or maybe even a rebuke, a Bible verse, or a mild scolding. Instead, what he said was simple, humble, honest, and from the heart. He said as he smiled, something very close to the following, "I'll let you know when that happens for me."

Several years later, Jacob attended a senior-high retreat with the Grace youth group, and for the retreat they went up to Camp Patmos on Kelly's Island, one of the many Lake Erie islands in the Sandusky Bay area.

There were probably about 100 young people from the church at this retreat, teenagers away for a weekend, supervised and led by some really good and dedicated people. These included staff and some student volunteers.

Friday night was the opening, a time to get to know some of the kids and possibly set some tangible goals for the weekend. You know, like "Why are we all here and what do we want to do?"

Way back in high school at Elyria Catholic in about 1968, I went on a similar weekend youth retreat called the Search. We spent the weekend listening to talks by parents, priests, older students, and some students our age. The purpose was to help us live out our faith and develop fellowship with our peers in the area of faith. It was also to train us in the area of faith. We stayed up late, talked a lot, hung out with the guys—and girls.

I was a sincere believer and really enjoyed the weekend. I also enjoyed the possibility of meeting one of the Rigali girls. I think there were two of them, or maybe I wished there were two. I believe one was Ann, dark Italian eyes and long brown hair, just very naturally beautiful. Her mom and dad were two of the main speakers, probably about 35-40, looked like movie stars, mom gorgeous, dad handsome. They were also super good Christian, faith-filled people. But it sure helped that they looked good.

Back at Jacob's retreat on Kelly's Island, the leaders and volunteers started going around the room and asking questions to each of the students.

"Johnny, what do you hope to get from the weekend?"

"Well, I hope to improve my walk with the Lord," says Johnny.

"Very nice," replies the staff member.

"Suzie," says a volunteer, "what are you hoping to attain this weekend?"

"I hope to learn more about the Gospel of John."

"We can help you do that," says a staff member. "That is a great goal."

This goes on for a while. Then they finally get around to Jake.

"Jake, how about you. What would you like to accomplish this weekend?"

"I'd like to have sex with one of the volunteers," Jacob replies.

Silence for a few seconds. But maybe not everywhere. News travels fast in the heavenly realms. Somewhere in heaven I envision an honest pastor shaking his head, but with a slight smile, as he enjoys eternal rest.

Bible Verse: " … he [Abraham] said to his wife Sarai, I know what a beautiful woman you are." Genesis 12:11

For Consideration: The ministry staff handled this situation very well. They didn't give him the attention that he most likely wanted, but let him know it was wrong, and then just moved on. As parents we have to continually work on our kids' filters. But, like the good pastor, let us not forget a good sense of humor!

Chapter 16

Mad Max

One of the ladies Jake has dated is named Olivia. They met through our Jacob's Ladder Special Needs Fitness exercise group. She is a pretty and sweet girl and has traveled far and wide as a model. Having Down syndrome has not stopped her from being successful, nor has it made her act differently in any way or become arrogant, even though she *has* been to Paris.

In about 2018, we were involved in a fundraiser for one of her model travel shows. It was at a very quaint little bacon-and-egg type restaurant . It was the perfect place for a Saturday morning breakfast, and the owners were helping Olivia's family with the fundraising. People were coming and going all morning, but they had it arranged so that they were not rushing anyone. We got to enjoy our meals.

We were all dressed like Saturday morning, very casual, no pretense. It could have been a pre-Saturday chores breakfast, or a post-Friday go out and stay up late thing. There were some sweatpants (that may have been me), baseball hats, sweatshirts, work sweatshirts, and medium-weight jackets. It was still a little chilly in Northeast Ohio.

Jake was with us. As mentioned, he and Olivia had dated several times and we got to know her parents John and Vicky. After we got our breakfast and were on our way to be seated, Jake noticed a young lady at one of the tables. She was sitting with a guy and having a conversation. She may have known Olivia and her family and was there to support the fundraising. Jake said hello and they exchanged pleasantries. She had a baseball hat on, very casually dressed, not all made up. Remember, it was Saturday morning.

Jake has always related well to females be it teachers, principals, education aides, nurses, volunteer Special Olympics swim ladies, etc. This ability has been part of Jake for as long as we can remember.So, Jake managed to get the name of the lady at the restaurant. Again, she was nice and polite to Jake, and seemed to speak to him like she would to anyone else, and that was appreciated.

After the fundraiser breakfast, we went home and Jake Googled her name. It was a little different than what we saw at breakfast. Turns out she was a *Maxim* magazine supermodel. She had been named *Maxim* girl of the month, or something like that, pictures verified.

Alrighty then.

Bible Verse: "Charm is deceptive, and beauty is fleeting, but a woman who fears the Lord is to be praised." Proverbs 31:30

For Consideration:

- Our special needs boys and girls are a lot like regular boys and girls and notice all the things typical adolescents do.

- Install appropriate blocking devices on all computers and phones and don't be surprised if your kids try to turn them off.

- No, we did not ask the *Maxim* model to lead any exercise classes for Jacob's Ladder.

- And, from Rocky, "Women weaken legs.

Chapter 17

50 Yards to Glory

Some of the all-time great collegiate sprinters in America have run at The Ohio State University track-and-field facility in Columbus, Ohio. This is where Special Olympics of Ohio holds the annual track-and-field finals. How awesome is that? It's one of the best college facilities in a beautiful setting.

There are about 2,000 Special Olympics athletes at OSU on that day, usually the last weekend in June. Also taking place at that time are the Special Olympics softball throw, bike riding events, powerlifting events, and bocce ball finals. These take place at other awesome venues at OSU.

To me the atmosphere at this track meet is like that of any high school or college finals meet. There are lots of events going on at the same time and the constant voice of the announcements of various events. "First call, men's 100-yard dash," comes over the speaker. As an athlete you get more psyched or nervous the closer your event gets, and each time the loudspeaker blares out the various events, you think, "We are getting close." Then there are the constant sounds of the starting guns going off and the athletes running to the sounds of cheering parents, friends, and coaches shouting, "Go. Suzie Go!!"

There are also athletes warming up all over the place, running, stretching, jogging, or just standing around waiting for their event, maybe drinking some water, then being told by the coach not to drink too much water before the race.

There are probably more coaches required for Special Olympics because some of these athletes can get distracted. One more reason why all these volunteers deserve so much praise.

If someone watched the faster heats of the 100-yard dash Special Olympics finals, they would think this was a pretty good high school track meet, and some of the stopwatch times verify that.

Sunday Special Olympics track practices back in Strongsville are not easy for these athletes. They are pushed somewhat, which is good for this population, the same as it is for typical high school athletes.

Jacob switched from the 100-yard dash to the 50 a few years earlier. He seemed to enjoy it more. The running was not quite as long, and he has a decent start. In 2019 we trained two to three times per week, in addition to the Sunday Special Olympics track practice. Our training facility was the road in front of our home. There are only 17 homes in our neighborhood and the road is a cul-de-sac about 200 yards in length. So the traffic is pretty light and the neighbors don't speed, for the most part.

One day per week we worked on starts. Jacob was taught the proper stance and how to place his hands right on the starting line. He worked pretty hard just on getting out of the blocks. There are not any starting blocks in Special Olympics, but we still worked hard on that aspect. So maybe we did 5 to 10 starts and just went about 15 yards. We worked on coming out low and driving, then keeping the head straight and pumping arms without letting them go side to side.

We also had days where we ran strides longer than 50 yards, say 60 or more yards. Jacob would run past our neighbor's house. He tried to run these at about three-quarters speed with emphasis on striding out and relaxing. Jacob worked hard. He was very tired afterwards, but stuck with it. I think we did this routine for about a month before the state meet. So he was in pretty good shape for the finals.

He also competed in and won the softball throw that Saturday. He had worked on the softball throw every Sunday at practice. He is very good at throwing. He is always the shortest thrower and goes up against some good athletes.

I am sometimes concerned he will hurt his shoulder, but his technique is very good. He gets his entire body into the throw.

As we got closer to the 50-yard dash final for Jake's group, we did our warm-ups—dynamic stretching, then worked up to some hard sprints. Then it was over to the tent to get into the competitive groups that he would run against. The athletes actually sit in chairs right next to their opponents.

"First call, 50-yard dash, division 456." I could see Jake getting psyched and nervous. It is like that when you actually sit next to your competition. You start to think, "This guy looks fast, and he is taller than me."

As the young men were seated in the tent, and we were getting very close to the race, I saw one of my buds from Prentice Autism named Dave. Dave is another one of those dedicated people who makes great efforts to support his athletes and goes the extra mile. Dave knows me and Jake and said hi to me and then told me he had a good athlete in the heat. He said the kid was fast and looked good in practice, and that he would compete well with Jake. And then, he said the words that would change the fate of this race. "And Tony," he said, "I have our prettiest volunteer waiting for him and cheering for him at the end of the 50-yard dash."

I worked very hard at not smiling, but I knew he had uttered the words of sure victory for Jake. Inside I was grinning broadly, just smiling for joy and thinking to myself, "Wait a minute, Dave. You are telling me that you have a good athlete here who is pretty fast, and you are putting an attractive young lady just 50 yards from my son?!" And here is the kicker, "You are asking Jake to run towards her? Fast?"

Have you ever heard of those dads who will do anything to get their kids to win? Sometimes stuff that is not really fair? This may have been a very coincidental version of that.

It was not close that day. Jake blew out of the blocks and won by 5 yards, maintaining good form across the finish line. I was very happy he did not go out of his lane to get to the volunteer lady.

Bible Verse: "Do you not know that in a race all the runners run, but only one gets the prize? Run in such a way as to get the prize." I Corinthians 9:24

For Consideration:

- How many athletes in the history of the world have been motivated by an attractive person of the opposite sex?

- Help your kids train for events, or use a personal trainer. It is great for them to learn to work for something and see the fruits of their labor. It is also good for learning how to be coached, take constructive criticism, and follow directions.

Chapter 18

For the Birds

There was an interesting thing about Jake's baptism, and something we did not expect. He is usually very averse to water that is sprayed or that rains on him. He never gets from the car to inside the garage as fast as when it rains. Then he motors like a sprinter! Karen and I may have threatened him with a spray bottle once or twice. I can't say we have ever done it. At least I don't remember us ever doing that.

He is also very afraid of certain birds, especially the smaller ones that flutter and fly around the yards in the summer. If one comes at him, or if there is a flock nearby, he kind of freaks a bit and takes off for the house. It's those tweety bird kinds of fliers that irritate him a lot. To his credit though, he has never used the bird thing as an excuse not to mow the lawn.

When Karen's mom came to live with us, we had to have the shower adapted for her in the bathroom that she and Jake shared upstairs. That involved the remodelers going through Jacob's bedroom wall, which was on the other side of the shower wall in the bathroom. The situation was that there was going to be an open hole in the wall in Jake's room for a few days with exposed pipes. We did not want his inquisitive and curious mind to lead him to exploring that hole in the wall, and we did not want him getting injured either.

So, Karen came up with an idea. She went and got a little fake bird and a small cage and put it right in the opening in the wall where the work was being done. I hope we did not cross some kind of line here, but he did not go near the construction hole, and did not complain. Good for him and us.

OK. So there was one other time when he was really misbehaving. I mean really bad. He would not listen to us at all and was acting out totally. Karen got the fake bird and put it somewhere he could see it, and then started making fake birdie sounds when Jake came into the room. We all laughed and teased him about it. He really was not amused at first, but smiled and laughed with us as the situation unfolded. And he ceased the bad behavior. I swear she only did that once, but I would of course never do such a thing.

Bible Verse: "Whoever loves discipline loves knowledge, . . ." Proverbs 12:1

For Consideration: Don't call the po-po on us yet. A sense of humor can be a powerful diffusing tool when disciplining any child.

Chapter 19

Nailing the Interview

It was fall of 2019. One of our Jacob's Ladder exercise sites at that time was at a large complex that years ago was the Cleveland Force soccer team complex. Now it housed an ice hockey rink, a workout fitness area, and another huge area for volleyball teams to compete. That area alone seemed almost as big as a football field, enough space for at least five volleyball courts, and plenty of area around the courts.

We were lucky enough to have the owner of the facility let us use it free, once a week for several weeks, to do our Jacob's Ladder exercise classes. The owner's daughter Lauren does a ministry called Grace Enabled, which also serves the special needs population. Lauren is also a dietician and a Christian with a heart of service. Along with her husband, Dan, they provide social and fun activities, like dinner dances with DJs.

We had been there several weeks when we got a call from the Spectrum TV cable company. They were interested in doing an interview with us and were going to film one of our exercise sessions for a segment on TV. Exciting stuff!

So, before the interview, we decided not to coach Jake too much on what to say if he was interviewed. Our only advice was tell the truth, be nice, look at the camera, and be friendly to the interviewer.

When the big interview night came, we arrived at the fitness center early to make sure all was well and we were all ready to go. The team from Spectrum showed up, and in our conversation before the interview, the anchor said she would interview me first, then interview Jake while I worked out with the other students.

I saw, or at least thought that there could be a problem with that. She was a very pretty young lady who wanted to interview Jake by himself, no mom or dad, just him. Immediately I thought of the following scenario. The lady starts to talk to him. He responds, but then the conversation changes focus. He asks her to come over to his house and have a glass of wine, just for the interviewer to visit with his mom, of course. Then he starts asking if she has a boyfriend or husband. Or, he says, "Would you like to meet my older brother who just happens to be single?" This could go in a whole lot of directions, none of which were good as I envisioned it going.

She talked to him for 10 to 15 minutes or so while I was busy exercising with the larger group. I kept looking over at them, thinking maybe she would get up and leave, or something worse. After the session, she very pleasantly thanked me and said she would send us a copy of the video. She also said that Jake did well, so I was somewhat relieved, but she never told me what he said. We had to wait to see and hear that.

So, as we watched the video, it showed Jake exercising in the plank position (our signature exercise), talking while planking, and saying that this planking thing was a "tough position to be in." He also said that exercise was good and that it made people strong and healthy and confident. Then he said, when referring to his having Down syndrome, "I am born with it, but it doesn't define me. Just like Rocky, a contender who refused to give up, but he kept on trying."

What!? Where in the Sam Hill did that come from? "It does not define me?!" Wow, Jake. You just completely shocked me and Mom! That was one of the most outstanding things I have heard any person say anywhere, son!

7:23 PM

I was born with it, but it doesn't define me. Just refused to give up, but he kept on trying.

Bible Verse: "A wise son brings joy to his father…" (and his mother!). Proverbs 15:20

For Consideration: I think I committed the mistake I have said parents of special needs people often do. That is, having low expectations. This dude really is special, and so are your kids.

Chapter 20

The All-Universe Wrestler

Jake was on the school wrestling team in junior high and early high school. He seemed to like wrestling, so we thought it might be good for him. Strongsville has a large suburban school system with a good overall athletic program and a very competitive wrestling program. And the coach was an Italian guy with a wrestling last name, so we liked him.

Anyone who has ever wrestled knows how difficult practices are in terms of conditioning. There is running, up-downs, push-ups, sit-ups, pull-ups, and weights, just about anything the coaches can think of to make it a grueling experience. Also included are the many rounds of rigorous wrestling matches with teammates as preparation for the meets. This is a very physically demanding activity and not everyone can do it.

I attended a few of the practices, and all the memories of my very mediocre wrestling career came back. Wrestling was torture for me. But Jake was hanging in there pretty well with the workouts and practices. Like many of his teammates, he was totally exhausted after practices, and it was not difficult to get him to bed on time.

I spoke with the coach, and he said, to my surprise, that Jake was very competitive and held his own at practice. We went to all the meets that year and Jake won a few matches. He was getting the hang of wrestling and liked it.

One weekend we attended a large meet of about 12 or so schools. It was one of those all-day Saturday tournament things. There was more than one gym involved and each gym had three matches going at the same time. There was lots of noise as parents, coaches, girlfriends, and teammates cheered their athletes on. Referee whistles blew constantly and there was the periodic referee slamming his hand loudly to the mat, telling everyone that someone was victorious via a pin.

Jake had wrestled a match and lost, though again he held his own. His next match was in the consolation rounds and was in one of the less visible gyms, with not a lot of attendees. His opponent was a studly looking wrestler who had obviously been beaten by a very good opponent. I could see that as they warmed up. The match began and I saw the opponent take Jake down with relative ease. Jake was fighting hard though and did not quit. He wrestled his way out of difficulty and began putting some moves on the opponent, pressing him.

As the match went on, I began to see a pattern. The opponent would take Jake down, then Jake would battle back and work hard to make a move to press the other young man. Then, just when it looked like Jake was about to get pinned, he turned the other guy on his back and pinned him. Smack went the referee's hand to the mat! He soon raised Jake's hand in victory.

But wait a minute. Something was up here. I saw what was happening. The other guy was letting Jake win, but not at all making it look obvious. At first, I was a bit miffed. I did not want Jake given anything. He had to learn how to lose, right? But then I started to think of what the young man had done.

After the tournament was over, I went and spoke to the young man's coach who told me the story. The young wrestler decided on his own that he would perform an act of kindness and encouragement for Jake. He told his coach that he wanted to let Jake win, but would not make it obvious and would make Jake work for the victory. The coach OK'd the deal and was so proud of his young wrestler's act of kindness and maturity. I shook the coach's hand and almost cried as I thanked the young man and told him what a kind act he had performed for our son. Might have given him a hug.

Bible Verse: "Therefore, as we have opportunity, let us do good to all people…." Galatians 6:10

For Consideration: This was a very thoughtful and kind young wrestler, truly an All Universe guy. He thought of another person instead of himself. What a blessing that there are so many people like that in this world.

Chapter 21

Anger Management

Is it possible that husbands and wives might occasionally have minor disagreements? Never, right? Not us. No way. Everything is just hunky-dory for Karen and me. OK, in truth, there may be times when we have words with each other, just like all couples. And those who have strong faith and strive to practice it still argue at times.

What we have in every marriage situation are two imperfect people trying to do their best to work out a successful marriage. Karen and I have been married over 27 years and have experienced the normal ups and downs of being married. In our case the dynamics include one emotional Italian man and one only occasionally stubborn German woman.

There are also data and studies that support the idea that middle-age parents of special needs children have greater depressive symptoms, more difficulties in activities of daily living, and an undermining of long-term health.

Whatever the cause, Jacob does not react well to these tense moments between me and Karen. He gets upset. Sometimes he thinks we are arguing when we honestly are just having a discussion. In those situations, we often let him know that we are really not mad at each other and hug each other, and then he calms down.

But one time we were going at it and there was disagreement and intense discussion. I'm not sure what the topic was of course. How many couples remember what their arguments were actually about?

As our argument progressed, or rather regressed, Jake got up and left the room. He stormed out of the kitchen into the family room and sat on the couch, then put his headsets on and began watching something on his laptop. As he left, he said something to me angrily under his breath.

Any time a disagreement happens, he always takes sides—with his mom. I love the fact that he does this. I really do. He has a strong mama protection kind of thing going. A while later we all calmed down and everything was back to normal.

Later that evening I got a little scriptural note from Jake on my office desk. Like an email, it was officially addressed to me and said "to: Tdorazio" and read, "He who is slow to anger is better than the mighty, and he who rules his spirit then he who takes a city." I contemplated the situation for a few minutes and was thankful for him, again. Yes, it was a little bit of in-your-face Dad, but obviously something I needed to hear, and after him hugging me, I knew it was sent with good intentions.

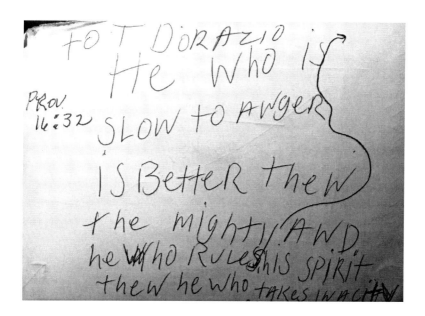

Bible Verse: "Better a patient man than a warrior, a man who controls his temper than one who takes a city." Proverbs 16:32

For Consideration:

I am very glad Jake is learning the Bible and communicating what he has learned, even if it hurts. Jake, and maybe others in the Down syndrome community, seem to have a very high level of ability to perceive when the people around him are experiencing anxiety. Again consider this awareness and empathy a possible gift.

Parents, if you're having problems with anger management, anxiety, or depression, don't be afraid to reach out to the many community resources available to assist you in finding counseling services. Your local church could be a good place to start, and there may be services available through your employment healthcare provider.

Chapter 22

Jake's Posse

Jake's family are without a doubt his closest friends in life. He grew up with many of them. They all have had a positive impact on him, and for that we are very grateful. Our families reflect the very best examples of how to treat any individuals, much of this is rooted in a deep faith in God. I will tell you the other aspect of the secret sauce of this at the end of this section.

Like many or most extended families, they were tentative with Jake at first, kind of not knowing what to expect. This was probably because we were too as parents, this was a new journey for all of us. As time went on, everyone came to realize and understand what he was like as a person.

The Wolf Family

Matt and Nick are Jake's first cousins on Karen's side. They had lots of sleepovers growing up. Jake loved the camaraderie with those guys. Karen's brother Greg is their dad, also a favorite. Jake called him Uncle Lugga for many years. Cousin Nick truly treats Jake like a younger brother, playfully harassing Jake over many things. Nick is also not shy about getting in Jacob's face if he gets out of line, especially if Jake is messing around in Nick's 4x4 Chevy truck with huge tires.

Perhaps most influential in that family was Greg's late wife, Joanne. She was kind and loving to Jake, but among other things, made him eat what he was served when he stayed overnight there. A very good lesson. And, this is huge, she taught him one very essential habit when he was very young. After you take a shower and are drying off, a good drying technique is the fanning method. Take the towel in two hands, put your legs wide apart, and fan your underparts dry. It had a great cooling effect. I can remember when he first showed us Aunt Joanne's technique. How pleased he was and sometimes shouted joy as he did it. The simple things, right?

Zach, Jordan, and Lucas D'Orazio

Everyone in our entire family has welcomed Jake and in many cases have worked with him on various aspects of his life. Uncles Vince and Dan have coached him in golf, uncle Rye connected Jake with the Fellowship Of Christian Athletes. Aunt Linda and her family pray for us regularly and are encouragers to Jake. All my siblings and many in our extended family have supported our efforts with Jacob's Ladder Special Needs Fitness. Cousin Madie Zofka is an exercise volunteer for the group. To a person, everyone is kind and interactive and shows respect and love to Jake.

Zach, Jordan, and Lucas are my brother Dan's sons. Jake spent a fair amount of time with these guys growing up too. He spent some vacation time with them, and did his share of sleepovers at Aunt Mary Kay and Uncle Dan's. He also grew up watching them play high school and college football. These three are all well-raised, God-fearing, and kind-hearted young men. They are also all football studs. All three were all-conference caliber players and beyond. Each played college football at Akron, John Carroll, and Duquesne, respectively, and Zach spent some time with the New England Patriots.

Zach, Jordan, and Lucas have always been friends to Jake. But, like any good friend, they give him a lot of good-natured teasing. OK, they give him a lot of stuff, the kind of stuff that we all do in our family and young men everywhere do to each other. They don't tiptoe around him having Down syndrome. They just treat him like one of the guys. In fact, a lot of times, they greet him by saying, "What's up you bum!" Sound hard? Not at all. Calling Jake a bum is like Rocky Balboa saying, "Yo, Jake, I love you brother!"

There is one other aspect to this that I am really glad about. I think about these three as kind of protectors of Jake as he becomes a man himself. Zach is a policeman. Jordan is a teacher and football coach. Lucas is a defensive end at Duquesne University as of this writing. All of them are good guys, but all have a switch that activates if needed. I'm pretty sure the switch would turn on to a high level if they thought Jake was in danger. I like Jake's odds if any one of the three dudes are in his corner. This also applies to their friends who know Jake.

Aunt Nancy

Certain people just connect with others for some reasons. Sometimes we don't know why. Karen's sister, Nancy, and Jake seem to have had that bond since he was very young. Nancy is our number one go-to person for watching

Jake and hanging out with him to watch his favorite TV shows (*Chicago Police* and *Fire and Med*—in that order).

Nancy was diagnosed with MS some 30 years ago. Nancy had been a cheerleader, standout softball player, and an overall active lady. A graduate of Miami University of Ohio with a degree in finance, she worked in the accounting and auditing area of a large bank and was very successful. She had her dad's keen sense of analyzing things, in this case financial figures. Eventually she could no longer work due to her MS. . She will tell you openly that, had she not had MS, she would not have known Jesus as Lord. Not sure her own disability was what bonded her to Jake, but they are buds forever.

Karen and I are so very thankful for her sister, Nancy. By the way, she is not afraid to correct Jake and counsel him if he needs it.

Brother Ray

Jake and his brother Ray are separated by 30 years and have different moms. Different, but yet similar in some ways. Probably the biggest similarity is their hearts. Both have true hearts for others. Both have that awareness of others who are in need and a willingness to help.

I remember Ray seeming to be shocked at the level of young Jacob's ability to communicate and especially his level of perception of other people. I think he may have thought that Jacob might be more like a silent invalid. Then he got to know Jake.

At one point in his life, Ray stayed with us for about a year. For that period of time, Ray had Grandma's old room just across from Jake's room upstairs.

Ray became a very positive influence on Jake and became his lifelong hero and friend. Ray always told Jake to listen to Mom and Dad. They shared texts and girl advice and sleeping habits and a bathroom. Ray's military background was a good thing: shower daily, get enough shut eye, no inappropriate texts, and don't forget to feed the dog. They went to Cedar Point one summer day and rode every single coaster ride together. Ray said when he left us that Jake was the most thoughtful person he had ever known. Ray also coined the Biblical name for our exercise group, Jacob's Ladder.

Lady Jordan and Jenna

Lady Jordan is nephew Zach's wife and Jenna is nephew Jordan's soon-to-be wife. Lady Jordan got her nickname to avoid confusion when referencing her and her brother-in-law Jordan. She is a nurse and Jenna is a school psychologist. Besides the obvious outward beauty of both, they are kind Christian ladies who have spent lots of time hanging out with Jake at family get-togethers.

They listen and interact with him in a positive way, but also give constructive feedback and let him know if he is edging towards inappropriate discussions. I can't think of two more positive ladies in his age group who can help him through many of life's hardest struggles, like broken hearts and losses of loved ones. They will also share the joyful life experiences with him, like playing bocce at family picnics, dancing at weddings, and celebrating new family births.

Jordan and Jenna have double dated with Jake to Cedar Point. Lucas and Jake double dated at a fancy restaurant where Lucas instructed Jake on the technique of properly seating your date and other necessary skills in a more formal setting. Lucas also rode with Jake on our tandem bike in our annual fundraiser event. Lady Jordan and Zach invited Jake to be part of their wedding. As you can imagine, that was a highlight in his life at the time. It was a large family wedding, lots of bridesmaids, dancing with your suit jacket off and just being with the ones you love.

So, here is the secret sauce. Treat him like a friend, tease him like you would any friend, brother or cousin, have normal conversations with him and expect him to do certain things. And give him a little grace in realizing he has some limitations, but not excuses!

Bible Verse: "A friend loves at all times, and a brother is born for adversity." Proverbs 17:17

For Consideration:

- One of the best things we can do as parents is help our children develop good family relationships. Reflect on the value of each of our own family ties and how we often look out for and take care of each other.

- For those parents who don't have the family thing going, build your own unique posse with friends, church affiliations, mentors, caregivers and the many supportive organizations.

Don't mess with the posse!!!

Chapter 23

The Big Tent Revival

We were hosting a graduation party for Jake's cousin Matt, one of his favorites. It was a summertime party and we expected 60 or so guests, including lots of family and friends on Karen's side.

The party was on Saturday and we all took off Friday to get things set up. This included many signs and pictures of Matt that Aunt Nancy made, various umbrellas, the food station inside our house, the drink station outside under an umbrella, signs in the front yard, cornhole games strategically placed in the shaded area, some cleanup of the bocce court, and a large 20' x 12' tent.

Karen borrowed the tent from a friend. We had some limited experience in putting this kind of tent up, but not a lot, and had not done it in several years. It was one of those that seems to have about 50 pieces of plastic framing for the corners and connections. Then there were about 75 metal hollow pipes of different sizes. These were about 3 feet long and connected into the plastic frame pieces.

Sounds a bit confusing already, yes?

There were five of us putting up the tent on the concrete basketball court that is in our backyard. This was the perfect set-up place. It would allow guests to sit and eat comfortably in the shade of the tent on a warm summer day in Northeast Ohio.

We started late that Friday morning, about 10:30 or 11:00. Karen's brother Greg led the operation. He later admitted he had forgotten how to do the tent set-up thing. It was fairly hot, not stifling, but warm. As mentioned, there were five of us, including Jake. The procedure was to put the various pipes together and at the same time put the tent over the frame.

As we proceeded with this strategy, it was apparent something was not going right. While trying to hold up the tent and put the metal frame underneath at the same time, we kept dropping either the tent or parts of the metal-piped framing. Each time a metal pipe disconnected from the other portions of the frame, it fell to the concrete basketball court, making a rather high-pitched clanging sound, followed by a metal-rolling-on-the-concrete sound. This was usually followed by another pipe falling, with another high-pitched clang on the concrete, followed by rolling-metal sounds. Kind of a symphony of clanging!

After several minutes, these metal musical sounds were followed with human cursing sounds. At first these were mild. Then they got worse and more blatant. The fun of working together and preparing for a great family event was quickly evolving into a very physically and emotionally draining scenario. My guess is that this went on for 30 or 40 minutes, and the sun was getting hotter.

We realized that the situation was getting out of control. Tensions were high, and harsh and hurtful words were sure to come next. Just like in the Anger Management chapter, I thought Jake was getting upset. So, we decided to take a break, go in the house, cool off in the AC, have some water or pop, and just relax.

I went in first and sat and Googled how to put up a tent. Lo and behold, there it was, a set of specific instructions for putting up a tent like the one we had. We relaxed for a few minutes and shared our info. I then realized something— Jake was not here. I went outside and checked around the heap of canvas and pipes that was the tent, then went to the garage. I was a bit miffed. How could he just walk away in the middle of a job? And, where was he? I then checked his room, thinking maybe he had had it with all the tension and retreated there. Then I checked the basement. Maybe he went down to watch video games and cool off from the heat. He was not there.

I started to worry and went back out into the backyard. I started to walk to the front of the house to look for him and he came walking towards me. Sometimes a man has to take things into his own hands.

He then said rather confidently and maturely, "Dad, I went to find some neighbors to help us with the tent and they are coming over." Well, sure enough, Jake walked up the street and recruited as many neighbors as he could find. He asked, and three neighbors came to assist us.

And they all came willingly. We put the tent up in about 15 minutes. We all had a good laugh, and I was once again so proud of that young man. Jake saw a situation, realized it was getting out of control, and on his own, did something to rectify it!

Bible Verse: "Iron sharpens iron, so one man sharpeneth the countenance of his friend." Proverbs 27:17

For Consideration: Sometimes our children see things and situations clearly and want to help. This act was one of maturity in reading a situation. It was as if Jake thought, "Well, these guys obviously can't handle this job. They need help. I'll go find them some." What joy in seeing a young man growing up!

Chapter 24

Scrambled or Over Easy

It was Mother's Day 2020. I woke up early as usual that Sunday, and there was an odd odor in my room. At first I thought our dog Carlos had done some business in the room, but I did not see him or any sign of it. I also checked Jake's room, and found out that he was already out of bed, which was unusual for this early.

As I walked into another bedroom and began moving about upstairs, the smell got worse. It smelled like maybe something burning. I then got a bit panicked and hustled downstairs to see what Jake had done. I knew he had done something that caused the burning smell.

Sure enough, as I moved quickly into the kitchen, there it was! The small red fry pan was on the stove. Something very black and burned was inside of it, and smoke was filling the kitchen. Jake was right there, standing in the kitchen a few feet from the stove, kind of milling around, as if everything was normal and he was going to get the salt shaker or something. I immediately took the pan off the stove, turned the burner off from the "high" setting, and pressed the fan button.

"Jake, what is going on?!" I said.

"I'm making Mom eggs for Mother's Day breakfast," he said, seemingly not aware of the whole kitchen-filled-with-smoke thing.

Inside this red fry pan, which was always my favorite, were the dark remnants of Jake's Mother's Day surprise. About half the pan was filled with what looked like a kind of black tar that had been stirred a little bit. It looked like something out of a monster movie, maybe black kryptonite or maybe that black yucky stuff from one of the *Spiderman* movies. Near the bottom of the black abyss was a slightly lighter-colored object, about the size of a quarter. That had apparently been the egg yolk at one point.

Jake and I cleaned up the mess. Soon after that, Mom came down and ate some cereal. She passed on the egg, but gave Jake a big hug and told him how much she loved him. Then we both rehearsed with him what to do to make sure this would not happen again and how to react if it did.

Bible Verse: "May your father and mother be glad; may she who gave you birth rejoice!" Proverbs 23:25

For Consideration:

- Enjoy and be grateful for the pure hearts of our children.
- Teach and coach kitchen and cooking safety.

Chapter 25

Mom, Dad, and Jacob's Ladder

Sometime when Jacob was 9 or 10, I began thinking about starting an exercise group for the special needs population of our area. I could see that Jacob was benefiting from the exercise that we had done together for several years and thought others could benefit as well.

I wanted to do something more to serve. That idea is a direct result of being raised by two parents whose lives reflected their hearts to help other people in the name of Jesus. No, they were not missionaries, not ordained, and never went to seminary or Bible college. They weren't professional counselors or social workers. They had no professional ministry and never started a non-profit group.

Our mother Grace was born in Italy and came to the U.S. at five years old. Her dad, Tony, had served in WWII for both Italy and the U.S. He and his wife, Adelina, settled in Cleveland and raised a fine family of five. There was lots of work ethic there as Tony became a cement mason and the sons learned that trade growing up. Grace worked at a local bank for a time and was known as a very dedicated hard worker. She later became a mom of five herself, as well as a housewife, great cook, and extreme prayer warrior.

Our dad Lou was a foreman at U.S. Steel in Lorain, Ohio. He had served in the merchant marines in WWII and survived being torpedoed. His ship was literally blown out from under him. He received a medal and recognition for saving another man's life. After surviving the war, he had a positive sense of appreciation that lasted his whole life. He was grateful to the Lord for sparing him.

For them both, the real change came when they went on a weekend retreat in the Catholic Church called the Cursillo. There they met Jesus personally and grew in their faith. They still never started a formal mission or even ever named what they did, they just helped people in need. For example, the Bible group they were in brought meals to those in need at Thanksgiving, without fanfare or even telling anyone.

Oftentimes growing up, there would be a person who came to stay with us for a few weeks or longer. Sometimes it would be a younger person in the family who was having trouble of some kind, maybe substance abuse. Other times it might be a friend of Dad's who was in need. Many times, there were people there for dinner who we did not know.

The Good Samaritans (Luke 10:30–37)

One of our all-time best and favorite family stories about Mom and Dad helping strangers took place around 1975 on New Year's Day morning. At that time, our home was on a dead-end road, due to the construction of a new highway. The road was Route 83 and used to be more of a rural route that cars traveled on at higher speeds.

Very early on this particular New Year's Day morning, a man was traveling southbound on Route 83. He had been out the night before, enjoying whatever party and drinking activity he was involved in. Heading south at a fairly high speed in the wee post-party hours of the holiday morning, he came over the hill just north of our home, and to his surprise, there was a dead-end there where a road used to be just a few weeks ago. Smash! He went into the fence that was right at the end of our driveway. Luckily, neither he nor his car was seriously damaged, but he was not in any condition to drive.

Meanwhile, in our house, Lou was getting up to go to work at U.S. Steel. He was meeting his boss and good friend Howard early that day. As he left the house well before sunrise, he saw the car that had smashed into the fence. Being a safety guy and ex-merchant marine, Lou immediately took action. As he looked at and into the car, he saw the man was not seriously injured and quickly figured out the guy had been drinking and had gotten himself into a pickle.

So, Lou helped the man get his damaged but drivable car out of the tangled fence, parked the car in our driveway, and walked him into our home. After he made sure this man he did not know was OK, he gave him a blanket and had him lie down on the couch in the laundry room, where the fully dressed man went to sleep. Not feeling the need to wake his wife up, Lou left for work.

No police were called, as Lou figured the guy needed a helping hand, not a DWI. Because of this rescue, he was late getting to work. When he arrived at the steel plant, he recounted to Howard what had happened. Howard knew Lou's good-heartedness, but quickly analyzed the situation. "Lou," he said, "you put a strange guy on your couch and left him there and did not tell Gracie!" Howard then ordered him to go home right away.

Back at home, Mom woke up and walked down the hallway into the kitchen—time for some coffee. She noticed someone sleeping on the couch as she walked through the laundry room. Immediately she assumed it was probably her son Dan sleeping on the couch, or one of her other sons who had dropped by and decided to stay. No problem.

As she began to look closer, she realized it was none of her sons, or anybody she even recognized! As the hungover man woke up and Grace fully realized it was no one she knew, she did the only logical thing that made sense to her and was part of her helping nature. She introduced herself to the man, listened to his story, encouraged him to be more careful, and then made him breakfast.

Not long after that, Lou arrived at home. Grace and Lou bid the legendary family figure farewell and sent him on his way. Imagine this man recounting this story to his own family and friends as the years passed, "…and then these people I never knew took me into their home, let me sleep off my inebriation, then fed me breakfast and said a prayer with me…!" What a great application of Matthew 25:35, "…I was a stranger and you invited me in…" Here is the beautiful part, neither Mom or Dad thought this was a big deal, just part of what they did.

So, their mission was to listen and be kind and to share the gospel that Christ loved us all. There was no perfection here, just imperfect people who loved the Lord, often serving other imperfect people who did not have a clue about God.

My mom is 97 at this writing. Recently we sat at her window at the care facility and were discussing her and our deceased dad's "ministry." Mother Grace is very happy though fairly forgetful about many things, like who her grandkids are and if any of us have seen her husband, Lou, who passed 20 years ago. She does not forget to eat her candy bars though, ever. But as she reflected on what they had done over 50 years ago, and contemplated what we were discussing, she looked at me and very clearly said, "We tried to be kind and not necessarily in a hurry to correct the person's issues."

What a concept. Show kindness to people, especially when they are hurting, even if they might be doing less than desirable stuff. Sounds like a carpenter we know from 2,000 years ago in Galilee.

Dad's funeral was in May of 1999 in Avon, Ohio. Keep in mind he was not a well-known person. He was not a politician or an owner of a major corporation, nor was he a famous national or local athlete. He never made a fortune in money, but lived in the great and eternal fortune of his faith and family.

The folks at the funeral home told us it was the largest number of people they had ever had at a wake. As the hordes of people came through the funeral line, many wanted to share a very personal story about how Lou and Grace had helped them in some way in their lives. Others wanted us to know how good of a friend our dad was to them. Each story was specific to the person. All of them reflected the heart of the grateful merchant marine who rescued and served so many people in his life and loved his family and Lord so well. We all laughed and cried a lot that day.

Of course, this was a huge tribute and reflection on our mom. She was the team member who did all the cooking and cleaning for the various people that her spouse brought home. Many times, he let her know in the afternoon that a "few people" might be coming home for dinner that evening. She also faithfully prayed for these people, and often she was the one sharing the gospel with the guests.

Jacob's Ladder

There are five of us children to Lou and Grace. All are imperfect in many ways, but all serve the Lord in some capacity, depending on how each is led and called. Mine just happens to be the special needs community, where the Lord placed me to serve.

So, sometime in 2010 I decided to start an exercise group for special needs individuals. We began at Grace and have expanded our service area. At one point we had exercise groups on the far eastside of greater Cleveland as well as the far west side. We are currently at Christ Church near our home in Strongsville.

Christ Church is another wonderful group of people serving the Lord through their congregation in various ways. Pastor Chet Beetler at Christ Church is Laurie Beetler's son (see Forward and chapter 8). They welcomed us with open arms and we utilize the full-sized gym at Christ Church. Pastor Dave "Doc" Collings leads the congregation, he and his very down to earth staff have made it easy for us to serve the special needs population. He also has helped me personally with a very difficult challenge.

Our goal is to serve the special needs population by providing regular exercise sessions and healthy lifestyle education. Even though there are many fine organizations serving the special needs population, there is still a lack of activity for this group as a whole. And that seems to get worse after high school. We also pray after every session and may also read a selected Bible verse. We want to remain faithful to our Christian faith and heritage and openly talk about our faith in Christ.

One moment in this whole journey with Jake and our pursuit of fitness came from a conversation I had with a college friend at an annual get-together we have attended since the mid 70s. She was a contemporary of mine at Ohio Northern and a college hall-of-fame athlete in volleyball and softball. She went on to teach special education physical education for 30 years.

This conversation took place when Jake was very young. She said, "Tony, do you know what the single biggest thing holding these kids back is…?" Well, I thought for those several seconds as I pondered the question. What was the answer? We don't love them enough, I thought. That must be it. Or maybe, there are not enough programs? That must be it. Yeah, not enough programs. Marianne then finished her statement with what surprised me—and may do the same for some of you. She said very clearly to me, "Tony, the single biggest thing holding these kids back is that we don't *expect* enough from them!"

Well, I didn't see that one coming. But over the years I have come to observe that in other parents, coaches, and myself. This is an important takeaway from this entire effort. Mark this down. Maybe make a large sign to remind yourself—**have expectations for my child.**

Yes, our kids have some limitations, for sure, but there are things, many worthwhile, meaningful, productive, profitable things that they CAN do. Jake will likely never play college football like his cousins, though it might be possible for him to become an EMT, which he really wants to do. But if he doesn't, he will work hard at those things that he CAN do, and learn to do them well!

This is also related to the famous saying of legendary basketball coach John Wooden, a saying that is on the back of our Jacob's Ladder business cards, "Do not let what you cannot do get in the way of what you can do."

By doing what our children *can* do, they can be successful and also use their gifts and skills to serve others at the same time. This is what we are striving for with Jacob's Ladder Special Needs Fitness.

Bible Verse: "Each one should use whatever gift he has received to serve others." I Peter 4:10

For Consideration:

- Thanks to our great parents who taught us to serve the Lord by serving others in need.

- And of course, thanks to the many volunteers and supporters of Jacob's Ladder, more than anyone they make this possible.

Chapter 26

Meeting an Old Friend

This is a follow-up to the story in Chapter 2 about Jake's birth and Karen's experience with the specialist doctor I call Dr. Bedside.

So, we don't harbor any ill will here with the doctor, because things have probably come a long way since then, in terms of how these situations are communicated. We are going to give him the benefit of the doubt and assume he had good intentions. And, it makes no sense to be angry about this.

By the way, in response to what Dr. Bedside said to Karen at his birth, Jake reads well, is very computer literate, has driven a car, is a high school graduate and a certified group fitness instructor for special needs people, is CPR certified, has been hitting a speed bag and heavy bag since he could walk, can do one handed pushups, is a yellow belt in Taekwondo, and a certified boxing trainer for a fine group called Down to Box. He also drives a golf ball close to 200 yards, can hit a pitched baseball, usually wins the 50-yard dash and softball throw at the Ohio Special Olympics, and most of all, throws an adaptive football extremely well, especially if he is a little mad at me. And, Dr. Bedside, he has dated a supermodel named Olivia, as well as a very pretty athletic and kind girl named Leah, and has other ladies that want to date him.

So, take that Dr. B.!

OK, based on that last comment, I will confess that, upon rare occasions, I have had thoughts and imagined a scenario in which Dr. Bedside is in the ring with one Jake D'Orazio, a.k.a. Rocky Balboa.

Here is the scene. Jake is about 24 years old, in prime shape. Very solid, square, strong shoulders and a wide muscular back. He is not really tall, but his punches do pack a wallop, especially to the opponent's midsection. Sound like a boxer we all know and love?

Jake has had real-life boxing lessons from Mike Richardson from Soza Fitness in Parma, Ohio, whom we affectionately refer to as Mr. T. Mike is an ex-marine who had expectations for Jake and let Jake know that in no uncertain terms. Mike is in Jake's corner for this fight, along with, of course, Mick Goldmill from the *Rocky* movies.

Jake and Dr. Bedside are mixing it up in the center of the ring. The fight is fairly competitive, though Bedside may be fading. One of the Rocky movie commentators present at this internationally televised fight opines to his partner, "I have to say, Tommy, Dr. Bedside does not look in the greatest shape for this fight. It might be possible that he did not expect this kind of a fight from the young contender."

Mick, who has been training Jake and Rocky for pretty much his and their whole lives, is getting frustrated. He shouts out from Jake's corner in that raspy old voice as he is slamming his hands madly on the canvas, "The body! The body! Go to the body, Jake!" Jake looks over and gives Mick a nod and a slight winsome smile, sweat pouring out from his body.

He knows what this means. He has heard it before. He then moves steadily forward and lands one of his powerful left-handed body shots (we have these on a film of Jake hitting our heavy bag). He pauses, then sends a 1-2 punch to the jaw. He strategically ducks and follows with a perfect thundering right hook to the body, finding the mark with a thud to the ribs, much harder than the first, devastating the opponent's entire left rib section. Just to be sure, Jake sends two or three more of these wicked, angry, thumping body shots to his opponent's body, maybe as a way of sticking up for the many others like himself.

Dr. Bedside gasps. His breath has been clean-blasted out of his lungs. Ribs may be damaged. He folds over, retreats to his corner, walking with a gimp, holding his ribs, with a painful expression on his face—like Apollo in the first *Rocky* film.

After the fight, Jake hugs his defeated opponent, then takes him out for some Chicken McNuggets. Jake treats. He invites his and Dr. Bedside's girl-friends, and Mick and Mike, of course.

Bible Verse: "Do not judge, and you will not be judged. Do not condemn, and you will not be condemned. Forgive, and you will be forgiven." Luke 6:37

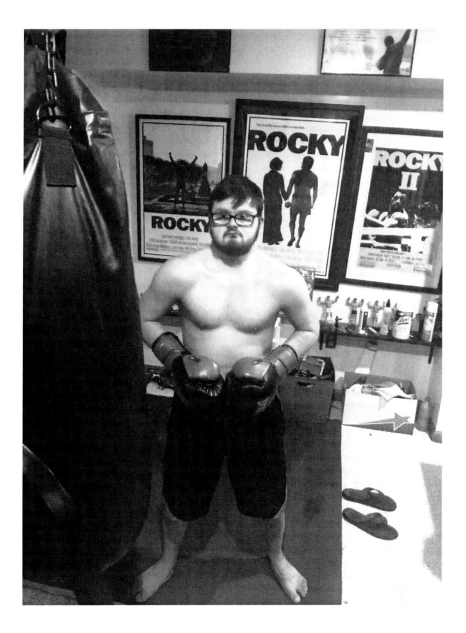

For Consideration: Just having some fun and letting off some steam.

Appendix A

It's Time to Move.
Parents, this is a must read section!

The obesity level in the special needs community is higher than the already high rate for the typical population. There is research to verify that. This was one of the motivations for me to write this book. I want to encourage parents to help their kids become healthier and more fit. That discipline will benefit them in all areas of life. And so, consider the following and make sure you consult your pediatrician initially.

First: Start young if possible. Getting into good fitness habits and routines early on makes a big difference. It also gets the child used to being coached and used to being able to handle some constructive instruction. **There is research showing that the single biggest predictive factor of any child's activity level is the activity level of the parents**. So, one of the best things you can do to ensure that your child is fit and healthy is for you to get fit and healthy and make it a family lifestyle thing. Put up a basketball hoop in the yard. Play baseball, football and other sports in the yard. Get your child into Special Olympics and become a coach.

But, if you did not start young, starting at any point in your child's life is way better than doing nothing. And it is beneficial, even if the person is overweight. The research also shows that exercise is good for those who are overweight or obese, even if they don't lose weight. And, consider how much easier it is to care for a person who is physically fit and mobile than someone who is not. All of you in my age group who are parents of special needs individuals are nodding and silently saying, "Yes. Yes!"

Second: Have expectations. Don't hesitate to coach your son or daughter on exercise technique, and definitely have some expectations. The single biggest thing a coach or parent can do to harm self-image is to ignore or dismiss a person because they assume that person cannot perform a task. It's good to say, "Do it this way son or daughter." Then demonstrate how the exercise is done and let them try. Then encourage, let them progress, make adjustments and keep moving forward. Hugs from parents are good too.

Don't hesitate to be enthusiastic and praise your child and motivate them to do better, as in, "Come on, girl, you can do this!" Remember, teaching skills and routines for any activities might take longer than for a typical kid. But don't give up. Keep making progress, even if it is small. It will come.

As an example, we started young with Jake with swimming, baseball, Ping-Pong, and exercising. Karen had Jake in the water when he was an infant. She had him hitting off the baseball tee when he was about four. We have pictures and videos of him smacking the wiffle ball from the family room into the kitchen.

For Ping-Pong, usually if someone comes over to play with Jake, they will begin by tapping the ball very easily and tentatively over the net. That is how we started over 10 years ago, but now it is just blast away. Hit it as hard as you want. Jake will play with you. The young man has very quick reflexes and an excellent backhand, even all his very athletic cousins will attest to that.

But we started slow with a smaller Ping-Pong table, hitting the ball very easily. Moms and dads, brothers and sisters, be prepared to chase a lot of Ping-Pong balls all over the basement early on (buy at least 50 Ping-Pong balls). Encouragement and patient persistence will work, this activity is great for hand eye coordination.

In the case of the speed bag, we had to put a bench in front of it to adjust the height so Jake could reach it. No problem, just a minor adaptation. When we put on some *Rocky* music or a *Rocky* training DVD, he would go at the speed bag with passion, and I did not have to chase the speed bag all over the basement like the Ping-Pong balls.

Most typical people can't hit a speed bag well at all and are usually at least mildly impressed with what Jake can do. They will almost always say, "I can't do that." It is the more serious athletes and boxers who really take notice, since they understand what is involved with this complex skill.

Speaking of expectations, when Jake was about seven years old, I guess, we had the talk. No, not about sex. That came later. It was the much more important talk about throwing the football. It was a nonnegotiable. I said, "Jake, if you can't throw the football in this family, I'll have to give you up for adoption."

OK, that didn't really happen. But the expectation, the progression and encouragement and coaching were there, and he answered the call. He does throw an adaptive football very well, especially if he is a little irritated with me.

Both Jake and I completed an Autism Fitness course. Important basic concepts were progression, which is making an exercise more challenging, and regression, which is making an exercise less challenging. Our planking information below is an example of progressing in an exercise. Research also shows that hitting a speed bag is used for certain patients with brain and cognitive issues. So, the speed bag routine helps the person get in shape, burns calories, greatly improves his or her reflexes and muscle tone, and improves their thinking process as well. Sounds all good to Jake, Rocky and me.

Jake is also a certified group fitness instructor through a great group in Texas called Special Strong. Daniel Stein and his team have a fantastic program, and they serve the Lord as well. I also got certified as a personal fitness instructor through this group.

Third: Start moving soon. Get into some kind of routine. Check with your child's doctor and maybe their physical therapist first. My prediction is you won't get too many negative responses on these activities. In fact, in most cases you will likely get a response from your doctor something like Rocky would say: "Go for it!"

Here are some simple options of things to do without any equipment and not that much time. Don't try and do them all on the same day.

- Walk around the neighborhood for about 20 minutes. Get into that routine and then increase the time. Invite the family and the dog.

- Have your child lie on the floor on her or his back and then have them get up to a standing position. Do that a few times, and then work up to more reps. It is kind of a reverse up down exercise.

- March in place. Put some marching music on. Do sets of 30 seconds to start.

- Have your child sit in a chair, and then get up. Repeat several times. This will help them learn to squat.

- Toss light weight balls or pillows or stuffed animals with them to develop hand eye coordination.

- Walk up and down the steps. Start with a few times and work your way up to several times. This can be a great workout.

- When they are old enough, have them take out the garbage and do other chores. Mowing the lawn takes a lot of steps.

- Run the vacuum cleaner. Our mom did this with the old heavyweight Kirby vacuum while watching Jack LaLanne over 60 years ago.

- One of my little sayings is **"Your home is an exercise facility; you just don't know it."** Besides what I have mentioned above, and with supervision and mom's permission, you can also do;

- Shoulder dips off the coffee table.

- Shoulder dips off steps.

- Plank using a wall to start if that works. Stand a few feet away from the wall, place hands on the wall in front of you at shoulder height and lean into your hands, elbows slightly flexed. As you get stronger, move feet back farther.

- The next progression could be planking facing the steps. The higher step you start planking on, the easier it is.

- As you progress, plank placing your hands on the bottom step with your feet back on the floor, you will be almost parallel to the floor.

- If you can progress beyond that, kneel on the floor at the bottom of steps facing away from the steps. Put your feet on the last step and plank outward, your feet will be higher than your torso. More challenging, you can keep putting feet higher on steps as strength is increased. This will take some time.

- Plank off the couch, start with the cushy middle section, then try putting your feet on the arm rest part.
- Planking is one of the best overall exercises you can do, it builds core strength. And, it's the signature exercise for Jacob's Ladder.

Teaching the youngsters, Jake and Kayla planking

- Do adaptive squats with your hands on the back of a stable chair. Then progress to regular squats.
- How about jumping jacks or just hopping around to start?
- Put a kid blanket between the couch and coffee table, then have the kids crawl through that tunnel.
- Do push ups. You can start on the knees with this exercise too.
- You may start with all adaptive versions of exercises, that is great. Start moving right away!

All these activities can be done playfully with the younger kids. Technique and proper form will come eventually.

In terms of equipment consider the following;

- A simple exercise mat.

- A yard trampoline, you will have to supervise and can join the fun.

- Various balls for tossing back and forth; tennis balls, rubber balls, volleyballs, smaller beach balls.

- Lightly weighted balls or bags for tossing.

- A ping pong table, start with a small table, then progress.

- Resistance bands, you can get the kind that fit into a closed door or on a door handle in the house.

- Some dumbells and weights as your child gets older.

- The larger exercise balls that you can sit on, these come in smaller sizes as well.

Use any equipment you have to set up an exercise area in your home, you can add equipment as you go, then work out with your kids, it will be good for all of you.

Bible Verse "In all toil there is profit, but mere talk tends only to poverty." Proverbs 14:23

For Consideration: Enjoy your children and the journey. **Encourage** your child. **Expect** them to do certain things.

Zoom Class 2020 Row 1: Jake, Sara, Emily, Peter, Tiffany Row 2: Tim, Cameron, Upton, Mel, Curtis & Charlie, Row 3: Carmen, Hudson Kayla & Avery, Cody, Maddie, Mick, Row 4: Brad, Jason, Deanna, Sophie, April, Row: 5: Deborah

Appendix B

Considerations

Much of what is said in this book relates to our experience with a child with Down syndrome, since that is what we know. I do think much of it applies to other types of special needs. Though I am not an expert on all kinds of special needs, I do have the insight of having done our Jacob's Ladder Special Needs Fitness exercise program for over 10 years. We have served individuals with many different types of special needs.

Early on, parents may want to give the immediate and extended family members some info on the specific special needs of the child when he or she is very young, kind of an overview. I think that a lot of people just don't know what to expect. So, we as parents should educate ourselves and then help our families learn about our child's particular situation. Maybe the format for this would be some kind of ceremony to announce your child has Down syndrome, or any other condition, kind of like they do now for the gender reveal parties.

As the child gets older, another aspect of this would include giving some specific instructions to family caregivers when the child stays with them.

When your child enters school, there is a whole new area of information for you to learn. It is especially important for parents to know what the expectations and options are for your child and for the school system they are enrolled in. There are absolutely many wonderful and dedicated special needs educators and administrators in our school systems. There are also organizations and groups that can serve as advocates for your child.

Moms, you may have to go into mama bear mode at times as you navigate your way through the school system and want to do the very best for your child. Again, lean on other parents and groups of people who have successfully navigated this area. You might also want to check out some legal resources.

And dads and moms, caregivers, sisters, and brothers, make sure you physically play with your kids with Down syndrome and other special needs. Unless the doctor says otherwise, roll around with them on the family room floor when they are young. Play catch with stuffed animals and throw pillows, hug them, kiss them, laugh with them, and tease them. What I am saying is do not treat them too delicately, and enjoy the heck out of your kids.

Early on in our adventure, when Jacob was an infant, we met with a family doctor who was a very nice pediatrician specializing in the area of higher-risk children. Karen, the doctor, and I were having a conversation about Jacob and some of the challenges we would face. At one point in the conversation I told the doctor that there would be no way Jacob would be inactive physically. I would make sure that did not happen. Then I looked directly at him and said, "Doctor, it does not matter to me. I will love him and spank him just like a regular boy." Karen is still embarrassed when I mention this, and the doctor had a kind of odd expression on his face after that comment. Later on, I thought that he might have been considering calling the authorities on me. But the point is that I committed early on to keeping Jacob active and it has worked for the most part. Ok, we never spanked Jake, but he did get his share of time outs.

So, teach your kids to play ball in the backyard. Show them how to throw a football and baseball. Take your kids on a date and coach them in sports and life. Teach your children to golf, ski, or play any other sport you like. Exercise with them regularly! I will repeat that another way. Be active with your children. That is one of the best gifts you can give them.

And, as they grow up, don't forget to teach them those key skills about taking out the garbage, mowing the lawn, doing the dishes, running the vacuum, folding clothes, cleaning the bedroom, and straightening the man/woman cave.

And you best be like any dad of a typical girl when your daughter with Down syndrome starts dating. Yes, maybe make that special needs guy she is dating a little on edge. Ask him the same questions and have the same expectations you have for the young man dating your other typical teenage girl. And most of all, parents, accept the blessed joy of having a child who might be the most sincere, honest, and caring (though occasionally stubborn) person you will ever meet in your life. Get to know your son or daughter as an individual. That may be the most rewarding and fun part of this new life trip you are on.

If you are a believer in Christ, rely on Him for help and strength. Rely on other believers as well. Remember what He said about the little children in Matthew 18: 2–5, "Truly I say to you, unless you are converted and become like little children, you will never enter the kingdom of heaven. Whoever then humbles himself as this child, he is the greatest in the kingdom of heaven." I think our children are an embodiment of this verse.

Jesus has been there for Karen and me, and is there for you. Just humbly invite Him into your life.

Bible Verse: John 6:40 "For my Father's will is that everyone who looks to the Son and believes in Him shall have eternal life, and I will raise him up at the last day."

For Consideration: Resources after pics

Joyful son and dad circa 2018.

Appendix C

Organizations and Resources

Jacobs Ladder Special Needs Fitness

Area: Northeast Ohio based, national for Zoom

Core business; Physical training and group exercise for the special need's community. Prayer after every workout. One on one personal training. Encouragement for parents, including weekly Bible studies and Zoom exercise classes. Christian based.

Website: www.jacobsladderfitness.com

Contact info: Email jacobsladderfitness@gmail.com
Phone 440 225 2365

The Upside of Downs

Area: Northeast Ohio based.

Core business; Provides individuals with Down Syndrome, their families and the community advocacy, support, and education.

Website: www.theupsideofdowns.org

Contact Info: Rich Tamulewicz- New Parent Support Coordinator- *Email:* rich@usod.org or Call: (216) 447-8763 X152

Awakening Angels

Area: Northeast Ohio based

Core business; Funds research, initiatives, and programs that improve child and adults with Down Syndrome and Autism life.

Website: www.awakeningangels.org

Contact Info: Email: getinvolved@awakeningangels.org or Call (216) 221-3992

Youth Challenge

Area: Northeast Ohio based

Core business: Provides sports and recreation to youths with physical disabilities with the help of teen volunteers.

Website: www.youthchallengesports.com

Contact Info: Email: yc@youthchallengesports.com or Call: (440) 892-1001

SOAR Special Needs

Area: Kansas based, national presence.

Core business: To provide families with disabilities resources, activities, and environments that are key to thriving in their local and faith communities as Jesus intended it to be.

Website: https://www.soarspecialneeds.org

Contact Info: Email: info@soarspecialneeds.org or Call: (816) 506-1305

Key Ministry

Area: Northeast Ohio based, National scope

Core business: Helps churches serve their families with disabilities more intentionally by providing resources and trainings for pastors and minister. They are help the families get connected with a church as well as providing them with helpful resources.

Website: https://www.keyministry.org

Contact Info: Call: (440) 384-0186

Down to Box

Area: Multiple locations

Core business: Through boxing Down to Box is able to teach individuals with Down Syndrome coordination, self-defense and fitness.

Website: www.downtobox.org

Contact Info: Call: (302) 709-1677

Global Down Syndrome Foundation

Area: Globally

Core business: Educates the government, organizations and society through research, medical care, and advocacy to improve the quality of life for people with Down Syndrome.

Website: www.globaldownsyndrome.org

Contact Info: Email: info@globaldownsyndrome.org or Call (303) 321-6277

National Down Syndrome Society

Area: Nationally

Core business: Supports and advocates for resources, support, polices, advocacy, and community relationships for people with Down Syndrome.

Website: www.ndss.org

Contact Info: Email: info@ndss.org or Call: (800) 221-4602

Special Strong

Area: North Dallas, Southeast Houston, Texas

Core business: Adaptive and inclusion fitness training for people with mental, physical, and intellectual disabilities.

Website: www.specialstrong.com

Contact Info: (833) 543-3496

Autism Fitness

Area: Worldwide

Core business: Fitness and adapted physical education programming and certifications for professionals that serve people with Autism and their families.

Website: www.autismfitness.com

Contact Info: Email: info@autismfitness.com or Call: 1 (929) 260-0686

Rec to Connect

Area: Northeast Ohio

Core business: Through recreation therapy programming they connect people with disabilities and their families to leisure skills, wellness, and recreation in the community to create a better quality of life for them.

Website: www.rec2connect.org

Contact Info: Email: admin@rec2connect.org or Call: (330) 703-9001

PALS Program

Area: New Jersey based, national camp locations.

Core business: A camp for people with and without Down Syndrome.

Website: www.palsprograms.org

Contact Info: Email: support@palsprograms.org or Call (267) 477-7257

Autism Spectrum Resources for Marriage & Family, LLC

Area: Through Zoom

Core business: Counsels couples and families that have a family member with special needs.

Website: www.holmesasr.com

Contact Info: Email: dr.stephanie@holmesasr.com

Air Weaver Balloons (The guy who was Thunderlips!)

Area: Sunbury PA

Core business: Entertainment and decoration for parties, events, parades.

Website: airweaverballoons.com or Call (570) 765-4535

Grace Enabled

Area: Northeast Ohio Based

Core business: A nonprofit that organizes free activities for people with special needs.

Website: Facebook: facebook.com/graceenabled/?ref=page_internal

Contact Info: Email: graceenabled139@gmail.com

In Remembrance

The year 2019 was difficult for many of us in that we lost several young people in the special needs community. We wish to remember and pay tribute to those who passed and meant so much to all of us, and who were part of Jake's circle of friends.

Myles Ketterer November 1, 2001 (All-Saints Day) - March 20, 2019

Myles Ketterer loved polka music, elevator rides, root beer and church. He laughed uncontrollably at burps and farts. Myles was a miracle in slow motion, he was (and still is) a catalyst for positivity. In his 17 years, he never allowed others the opportunity to just focus on his hardships, his limitations or disability. With a smile, he would force others to commit their full attention to who he was. He was a bright light. His gift was the ability to make everyone he encountered feel special and taught so many how to be fully present in a moment with others. Included in this group is Jake D'Orazio, one of his many friends from high school. The #mylesrippleeffect will forever spread joy and light to others. His light and love live on in the joy he shared with the world.

* * *

Albert Waters, Nov. 20, 1998 - Jul. 22, 2019

Albert came into the world the 7th child of a 26yr. old. mother exposed to drugs and alcohol. He was placed in county custody and was adopted into our family at 19 months of age. Albert got to know Jake D'Orazio through the adapted sports programs run by the Achievement Centers for Children and through Jacob's Ladder Fitness program. Albert's life was so enriched by these activities and he loved being a part of them and especially loved the friendships he made as a result. At the time of his sudden death in July of 2019, he had graduated high school from STEPS Academy and was working full time at The Learning Farm in Amherst, Ohio.

* * *

Michael Stanfield October 18, 1992 – February 2, 2019

Our son Michael came to us when he was 8 years old, along with his younger sister Stefanie. Little did we realize the trials and joys to come our way. Raising an Autistic child was not easy, but the love that he showed us was amazing and made it all worthwhile! Michael grew emotionally and physically, and his love for all people grew exponentially. He was a very kind, loving and gentle person. With a true Christian heart, he put others before himself.

Michael made friends wherever he went. When you were his friend, he stayed true to you forever. He absolutely loved his Special Olympics family and could not wait to be with them. There were many events he would go to, including Jacob's Ladder, Glee club, bowling, track and basketball. He never let his disability limit him, earned dozens of Special Olympics medals, became an Eagle Scout and was one of the best men we have ever known.

God knows we will dearly miss him. We often wonder what he would have achieved in this world. God bless you, Michael. You have made our lives much richer for knowing, loving and being loved by you.

* * *

Mikey George December 3rd, 2002 – June 23, 2019

A vibrant, loving personality with a contagious spirit, Mikey George lived a legacy that transcended his time on earth. Michael was diagnosed with Down syndrome when he was born on 12/03/2002 as the triplet brother of David and Julia. Like most parents who give birth to a special needs child, his parents Tony and Kristine, were forever impacted by Mikey's arrival. Many emotions overcame them as they turned to family, friends, and especially, The Lord for guidance. They moved forward from the early heartaches of Mikey's life to realize that his birth was the greatest blessing they would ever receive.

Mikey was a proud St. Edward Eagle and a dedicated Michael Buble' and Roman Reigns fan. Mikey entertained all with his singing and dancing at family parties and get-togethers. The creative nicknames he gave people were witty, clever, and memorable. He spent his favorite summers on Kelly's Island, where he enjoyed a no boundary lifestyle.

Mikey inspired many incredible organizations and initiatives including the Michael T. George Center at Welcome House, the Michael T. George - Saint Andre's Scholars Program, the Down Syndrome Research Center at Case Western Reserve University and University Hospitals headed by Dr. Alberto Costa and Awakening Angels – An organization committed to transforming the lives of children and adults with Down syndrome and Autism. The relationships and bonds that Mikey forged during his life are forever remembered by those closest to him.